Beyond the Arab-Israeli Settlement: New Directions for U.S. Policy in the Middle East

R. K. Ramazani

Foreign Policy Report
September 1977

INSTITUTE FOR FOREIGN POLICY ANALYSIS, INC.

Cambridge, Massachusetts

Requests for copies of IFPA Foreign Policy Reports should be addressed to the Circulation Manager, Foreign Policy Reports, Institute for Foreign Policy Analysis, Inc., Central Plaza Building, Tenth Floor, 675 Massachusetts Avenue, Cambridge, Massachusetts 02139. (Telephone: 617-492-2116) Please send a check or money order for the correct amount along with your order.

Standing orders for all Foreign Policy Reports will be accepted by the Circulation Manager. Standing order subscribers will automatically receive all future Reports as soon as they are published. Each Report will be accompanied by an invoice.

IFPA also maintains a **mailing list** of individuals and institutions who are notified periodically of new Institute publications. Those desiring to be placed on this list should write to the Circulation Manager, Foreign Policy Reports, at the above address.

Manuscripts should be submitted to the Managing Editor, Foreign Policy Reports, at the above address. They should be typed double-spaced; footnotes, also double-spaced, should be placed at the end. Manuscripts should be from 80 to 120 pages, or from 20,000 to 30,000 words, in length. Those not accepted for publication will be returned only if adequate postage has been provided by the author.

A list of IFPA publications appears on the inside back cover.

The Institute for Foreign Policy Analysis, Inc., incorporated in the Commonwealth of Massachusetts in 1976, is a publicly-supported, nonprofit, tax-exempt corporation, as described in Section 501(c)(3) of the Internal Revenue Code. Contributions to the Institute are tax-deductible.

Price: $5.00

Library of Congress Catalog No. 77-87564

ISBN 0-89549-006-4

First Printing
Printed by Corporate Press, Inc., Washington, D.C.

To Judge Hardy C. Dillard
for showing me the way

Contents

Preface and Acknowledgments

United States policy in the Middle East urgently needs rethinking. The Arab-Israeli war of October 1973, the Arab oil embargo, the explosion of oil prices and subsequent developments have created new realities, intensified old problems and produced new opportunities. Yet our ways of thinking, our attitudes and our assumptions have undergone little, if any, change. We have tended to equate the problems of American policy in the Middle East with the Arab-Israeli conflict; we have divided Middle East problems into artificial compartments of the Persian Gulf and the Arab-Israeli zone; and we have made studies, proposals and recommendations as though such problems as the conventional arms race, nuclear proliferation, and rival superpower naval deployment and base-building in one part of the Middle East have no relationship to basically the same problems in another part of the area. Furthermore, we have acted on the basis of earlier notions of containment as expounded in the Truman and Eisenhower doctrines, and in the newer tenets of detente and the Guam Doctrine, without seeking to clarify the interrelationships of these concepts and their bearing on our current and future interests and policies in the strategic Middle East.

Conceptual ambiguities in our Middle East policy have been compounded by perceptual traps. In trying to define our interests, to select objectives, to plot courses of action, and to evaluate the outcome, we have been inclined at times to look at the regional environment excessively from the outside in. Hubris has sometimes distorted our conception of the national interest. We have tended to define the Middle East situation in dangerous disregard of the realities of the region's societies; we have been prone to perceive the interests, objectives and priorities of Middle East countries in terms most familiar to us; we have too often compartmentalized their domestic and foreign policies so that we understand neither adequately; and we have at times evaluated the outcomes of their policies so ethnocentrically that we have, in effect, ended up condemning their actions in the jargon of the social sciences. The combination of conceptual ambiguities and perceptual traps lies at the heart of our repeated and sometimes unnecessary surprises, such as the outbreak of the 1973 Arab-Israeli war.

At the time of this writing (April 1977) the new Carter Administration has been in office only a few months. It has accorded high priority to Middle East peace; outlined the basic elements of a settlement; and declared that it is "terribly important" that progress be made toward a settlement and that "it be made in 1977." As contrasted with former

Secretary of State Henry Kissinger's step-by-step diplomacy, the new Administration's approach has been characterized as "comprehensive." But it is doubtful at the moment that this Administration believes any more than its predecessor that there is a great and urgent need for thinking about U.S. Middle East policy in a much broader and deeper context than the confines of the Arab-Israeli conflict. This study will argue that the United States needs a genuinely comprehensive, coherent and realistic conception of its overall policy in the Middle East. It will also try to indicate how progress toward such a conception could be made by asking two sets of questions. First, we must ask questions about the basic premises of our own policy in the Middle East. And second, if we are to gain a better understanding of the environment in which American policy operates, it is equally important to raise questions about the salient features of Middle East society and foreign policy.

Some of the ideas explored here are the product of many years of teaching, research, writing and consulting on the Middle East. But this is the first time that I have tried to synthesize these ideas and relate them to U.S. policy in the whole region. I would like to acknowledge gratefully the encouragement of my friend and colleague, Professor Kenneth W. Thompson, for reading the entire manuscript and offering helpful comments. Dr. Robert W. Stookey's encouraging reaction to a few of the ideas reflected in Chapter IV is remembered with gratitude. My indebtedness to Ambassador L. Dean Brown is also duly acknowledged on the brief section on Lebanon. I would also like to express appreciation to Professors Clifton McCleskey and David C. Jordan for their support of my travels in the Middle East. However, I am solely responsible for the facts and interpretations found in this study.

R. K. Ramazani

1.
The Problem

As ANTICIPATED, the Carter Administration launched its search for a Middle East settlement shortly after the inauguration of the President. On March 9, 1977, President Jimmy Carter publicly signaled what might turn out to be the general outline of his conception of a Middle East settlement.

Approximately one year earlier, in March 1976, the peacemaking efforts of former Secretary Kissinger had come to a halt, reportedly because of the Lebanese civil war. As a matter of fact, however, the principal reason for the stalemate had been the acrimonious rift that developed between Egypt and Syria over the Egyptian-Israeli agreement of September 1975, generally known as the Sinai II agreement. Kissinger viewed this agreement as the crowning achievement of his step-by-step diplomacy. In defending it against the attack of his critics, he stated: "I consider this agreement more significant than the previous two disengagement agreements that received much less criticism. It certainly gained some time for the peace process, and it may open the door to a general peace settlement." He also claimed that both Prime Minister Rabin and President Sadat hailed the agreement as a possible "turning point." The former Secretary himself added that it represented "the most far-reaching practical test of peace—political, military, and psychological—in the history of the Arab-Israeli conflict."[1]

The critics of the step-by-step approach, however, thought differently. One of the most persistent critics of step-by-step diplomacy, George W. Ball, the former Under Secretary of State and U.S. Representative to the United Nations, attacked the whole approach. He stated that it represented

an effort, through bilateral diplomacy, to make a little progress here, a little progress there, almost like following the stream of a river in an unknown terrain not knowing whether you're going to run into a cul de sac in the mountains or find another stream that takes you elsewhere. Not being totally sure about where you come out at the end.

An "indispensable" condition to a final settlement, according to Ball, was one in which the United States and the Soviet Union were in accord. "I don't think we can have a settlement," he stated, "in which the Soviet

---

[1] Department of State, *The Secretary of State*, September 9, 1975, pp. 5-6.

Union is totally left out and frustrated because with the beachhead they already have in the area I think they would continue to be a source of disequilibrium."[2]

Like George Ball, former Senator J. William Fulbright feared that

if the interim Sinai agreement is not soon followed by other, more substantial steps—especially with respect to the central question of Palestinian rights—frustrations will increase and tensions will rise; moderate Arab leaders will either be radicalized or displaced; and a fifth war will follow.[3]

But Fulbright, as contrasted with Ball, blamed domestic politics for the failure of American policy to achieve a comprehensive settlement. He claimed that

the key to peace in the Middle East is in the internal politics of the United States. As long as the Israeli lobby retains its extraordinary power to mobilize large majorities in Congress, the executive will be accordingly hobbled in any efforts it may care to make to bring the Middle East antagonists to a peace based on Security Council Resolution 242. As long as Congressmen and Senators are unwilling to face the political risk, possible loss of campaign contributions, and personal unpleasantness of well-organized pressure campaigns, we can expect little in the Middle East except deadlock, terrorism, tedious negotiations with little if any result, and in due course, sooner or later, the fifth Arab-Israeli war.[4]

Edward R. F. Sheehan, a close and sympathetic observer of Kissinger's step-by-step diplomacy, credited him with conducting "a diplomatic odyssey unequalled in our time," but he also criticized the tactical nature of the step-by-step approach.

If Arafat is like a cyclist atop a tightrope, Kissinger is like a lumberjack leaping from log to log, wishing that the river will lead him somewhere else. He suffers, by his own admission, from the syndrome of success; though his tactics have been brilliant and his techniques, too, strategically he has sinned on the side of caution.[5]

The former Secretary's alleged sin was his failure to address "the central issues of the Arab-Israeli conflict such as the future of the Palestinian people, and those issues cannot be postponed much longer." Sheehan, as contrasted with Fulbright, did not blame the Israeli lobby alone for America's failure to formulate a comprehensive Middle East policy, al-

---

[2] Department of State, Bureau of Public Affairs, News Release, March 6, 1976, pp. 4, 7. (Hereafter cited as DOS, News Release).

[3] Address by J. William Fulbright, "Beyond the Interim Agreement," The Middle East Institute, October 3, 1975, p. 17.

[4] *Ibid.*, pp. 36-37.

[5] Edward R. F. Sheehan, "Step by Step in the Middle East," *Foreign Policy*, Spring 1976, p. 69. See also his *The Arabs, Israelis, and Kissinger: A Secret History of American Diplomacy in the Middle East* (New York: Reader's Digest Press, 1976).

though he did admit its influence. He stated that the U.S. government's reassessment of its policy, announced subsequent to the breakdown of the Secretary's peace mission in March 1975, produced three options. The first of these, which he seemed to favor, was that the

United States should announce its conception of a final settlement in the Middle East, based on the 1967 frontiers of Israel with minor modifications, and containing strong guarantees for Israel's security. The Geneva conference should be reconvened; the Soviet Union should be encouraged to cooperate in this quest to resolve all outstanding questions (including the status of Jerusalem) which should be defined in appropriate components and addressed in separate subcommittees.[6]

The death blow to this option was apparently dealt by the "Israeli lobby," according to Sheehan. The lobby seemed triumphant when, on May 21, 1976, seventy-six U.S. Senators wrote collectively to the President to endorse Israel's demand for "defensible" frontiers and massive economic and military assistance. "At about this time," Sheehan states, "Sisco, Atherton, and Saunders unanimously advised Kissinger that the first option had no hope of surviving the counterattacks of the lobby—that now the administration had no choice but to resume step-by-step diplomacy."[7]

In December 1975, the members of the Brookings Middle East Study Group called for a comprehensive and phased settlement of the Arab-Israeli conflict. This study was reportedly influential in President Carter's statement of March 9, 1977, on a Middle East settlement. Although the Group believed that the conclusion of the Sinai agreement was undoubtedly "significant and useful," it brought out certain difficulties in the interim-steps approach. These included the Egyptian and Israeli perceptions of having made very substantial concessions, which made it politically difficult for them to make further concessions; the consequent divisions and recriminations among the Arabs that had complicated the process of settlement; the annoyance of the Soviet Union at being left on the "sidelines"; the congressional uneasiness at "growing U.S. involvement and commitments"; and the infeasibility, at the time, of negotiating either an Israeli-Syrian agreement or any kind of partial withdrawal on the West Bank. Having rejected any prolonged stalemate as an imprudent and unwise option because it would increase tension and could lead to renewed hostilities, the Study Group called for U.S. peacemaking efforts to concentrate henceforth on "negotiation of a comprehensive settle-

---

[6] Sheehan, "Step by Step in the Middle East," pp. 54-55.

[7] *Ibid.*, pp. 58-59.

ment, including only such interim steps as constitute essential prepara-
tions for such negotiation."[8]

The most fundamental characteristic of this undoubtedly important
study is its call for a "comprehensive settlement." The notion of "comprehensiveness" in the context of the study has two meanings. One is the
inclusion in negotiations of "all the parties to the conflict," that is, the
Palestinians as well as the others. The other is the consideration of the
"basic elements of the Arab-Israeli dispute" which, according to the study,
had still been left "substantially untouched," whatever the merit of the
Sinai agreement. These elements include the withdrawal of Israeli forces
from territories occupied in 1967; the acceptance of "secure and recognized" boundaries for Israel; Palestinian self-determination; and the
status of Jerusalem.

As far as it goes, the conception of settlement embodied in the Brookings' study no doubt represents an improvement over the step-by-step
formula. Its twofold comprehensiveness would make it possible to avoid
some of the pitfalls of the step-by-step approach. It includes all the parties
and all the essential issues involved in the Arab-Israeli conflict. As such,
implementation of its proposals could remove the kind of *ad hoc* and
piecemeal characteristics that marked Kissinger's peacemaking efforts,
which were largely responsible for the failure to address the core issue of
Palestinian self-determination and the problem of inter-Arab division
that was clearly aggravated by the acrimony between Damascus and Cairo
over the second Sinai agreement.

Yet, to the extent that the Brookings' conception of settlement over-
looks the wider and more fundamental Middle East environment of the
Arab-Israeli conflict, it is fraught with at least three major dangers. First,
since its definition of settlement is confined to the "essential issues" of the
conflict, it will create the twofold illusion that (a) a settlement can indeed
be achieved by addressing these issues alone, and (b) the entire Middle
East crisis will somehow disappear if and when such a settlement is
attained. The traditional tendency of at least the American public to
equate the Middle East crisis with the Arab-Israeli conflict is reflected in
this basic assumption, and is fertile ground for a new kind of misappre-
hension.

Second, the Brookings' conception of settlement tends to minimize the
magnitude of the problems involved in a Middle East peace settlement. As
we shall see, the Arab-Israeli war of 1973, the Arab oil embargo, the
explosion of oil prices, and the policies pursued since then by the United
States as well as by Middle East states make it extremely difficult, if not

---

[8] Brookings Middle East Study Group, *Toward Peace in the Middle East* (Washington, D.C.: The Brookings
Institution, December 1975), p. 7.

impossible, to confine the basic elements of the Arab-Israeli conflict to the issues directly in dispute between the "confrontation" Arab states and Israel. For example, the massive purchase of arms by the Arab states of the Persian Gulf in recent years raises seriously the probability of arms transfers from such states to the Arab states in actual armed conflict with Israel in any future war, and it can also complicate the processes of a peace settlement. Any kind of settlement will ultimately involve not only the recognition of Israel by the Arab states, the withdrawal of Israeli forces from Arab lands, the creation of demilitarized zones with U.S. guarantees as well as UN involvement, and an agreed status for Jerusalem and the Palestinians, but also some kind of an overall balance of power between the Arab states and Israel. The military element of that balance has become exceedingly difficult to calculate since the Arab-Israeli war of 1973, for in the intervening years the distinction between the "confrontation" and other Arab states has in effect been rendered obsolete by momentous events.

Third, and most importantly, the Brookings Group's neglect of the new Middle East environment of the Arab-Israeli conflict will adversely affect the shape of an overall settlement in the long run as well. It will tend to inhibit thinking beyond the stages of settlement, estimated by President Carter to take anywhere between two to eight years. To be sure, the President has also insisted on open borders and free trade and travel between Israel and its Arab neighbors, and President Sadat has responded favorably, but it is doubtful that such a requirement will usher in an era of "real peace," unless it is conceived within the context of two sets of much broader and more fundamental questions.

First, what kind of a regional order does the United States envisage for the entire Middle East? The disruptive impact of the Lebanese crisis of 1975-1976 on the processes of negotiations is a sobering lesson. It teaches that the Arab-Israeli conflict, or for that matter settlement, cannot be neatly separated from the adverse impact of other regional conflicts. There is no reason to believe, for example, that a conflict in the Persian Gulf can be confined to that area alone. In other words, we must begin to conceive the settlement of the Arab-Israeli conflict within the context of the broader need for a new regional order. Do we conceive of a simple "two-power" system or of a multiple balance of power system as a basis of future order in the Middle East? In either case, which states should be regarded as the major regional actors? If we are inclined to eschew the notion of balance of power as a means of achieving regional order in favor of the concept of regional cooperation, what degree of cooperation could we realistically expect and among which states? For example, do we envisage a self-contained collective security system among the Persian Gulf states to the exclusion of the now so-called confrontation states?

There are also other ideas of regional cooperation, such as Red Sea security, Indian Ocean Common Market, and collective security. How do we expect the "normalization" of relations between the confrontation Arab states and Israel to relate to these and similar ideas of regional cooperation in the future?

The second set of questions regarding the environment of the Arab-Israeli conflict is no less important. How stable will any form of regional order (through a balance-of-power system or regional cooperation, or both) prove to be in light of domestic revolutionary conditions in Middle East societies, where the interaction between domestic crises and external conflicts is far more acute than is generally recognized? Can any U.S. efforts to build peace and to encourage local powers to create a stable order produce durable results without massive American aid to, and patient cooperation with, Middle East governments—thus enabling them to meet the formidable social, technological and economic challenges of the future? And finally, what roles does the United States envisage for the Soviet Union, China and its transatlantic and Japanese allies and friends in the creation and maintenance of a future regional order in the Middle East?

These and similar questions are the important ones to raise in our search for a Middle East peace settlement, and they are pertinent to the twofold objective of this study: (1) to point out the urgent need for a comprehensive, coherent and realistic conception of U.S. policy in the Middle East region as a whole; and (2) to suggest the prerequisites of such a conception of U.S. policy extending beyond the confines of an Arab-Israeli peace settlement.

2.
The U.S. Response to the
Arab Oil Embargo

I N THE PRESIDENTIAL foreign policy debate in October 1976, Jimmy Carter declared that "if the Arab countries ever again declare an embargo against our nation on oil, I would consider that not a military but an economic declaration of war and I would respond instantly and in kind."[9] The argument of some observers that Saudi Arabia, which was singled out by Carter, would not resort to another oil embargo because of that country's overriding interest in its security and economic relations with the United States seems to make sense. But any such argument must be juxtaposed against the fact that, as long as the United States depends increasingly on Arab oil supplies, the possibility of an oil embargo does exist.

In fact, it can be argued that the Arab oil weapon would be more potent today than before. Arab states are in a much better position to embargo oil to the United States now than they were in 1973 when the total Arab share of the American oil-import market was 15 per cent, whereas it was 32 per cent for the first six months of 1976.[10] Furthermore, although the American-sponsored International Energy Agency (IEA) has set security against a new oil embargo as its primary objective, it is not certain at this time that its oil-stocking and oil-sharing programs would prove effective against a broad, as compared with a selective, embargo. A counter-embargo on shipments to the countries participating in an embargo could severely punish them (particularly Saudi Arabia), but such a far-reaching countermeasure would have little chance of effectiveness unless most industrial nations participate. The divisive problems of transatlantic relationships that surfaced during and after the October war do not provide a sufficient basis for optimism that effective collective countermeasures could be taken in the event of another oil embargo. Finally, we must remember that our belief in Saudi Arabian friendship, and our disbelief that the Saudis intended or would be able to embargo oil shipments to the United States, were in part responsible for our surprise in 1973—despite

---

[9] *New York Times*, October 10, 1976.

[10] The 15% figure represented only direct imports. If indirect imports were added the figure should be 17%. American oil imports from Iraq, Kuwait, Qatar, Saudi Arabia, Iran and the Union of Arab Emirates in 1973 amounted to 877,000 barrels a day. During the first six months of 1976 they amounted to 2,124,000 barrels a day.

repeated Saudi warnings as early as six months before the embargo was imposed.[11] We cannot afford to think about the future on the basis of already proven mistaken assumptions.

The circumstances under which another oil embargo may be imposed are impossible to predict at this time, but it should be remembered that both the imposition and the lifting of the Arab oil embargo have been linked to the Arab-Israeli war. That conflict still has not been resolved and there is no hard evidence that Arab states would deny themselves the use of an oil embargo in another conflict with Israel; hence, it is important to note that American peacemaking efforts were in fact tied to the lifting of the embargo, in spite of protestations to the contrary.

Peacemaking-Oil Embargo-Oil Price Linkages

The Arab oil embargo was imposed in response to the U.S. resupply of arms to Israel during the October war. On October 13, 1973, Egypt stepped up the pressure on King Faisal of Saudi Arabia to use his "oil weapon" against the United States. On October 17 the Arab oil states meeting in Kuwait decided to cut back production of petroleum destined for the United States, pledging a cutback of 5 per cent a month (raised to 10 per cent later) to the United States and other industrialized countries backing Israel, until Israel withdraws from the Arab lands it occupied in the 1967 war and "restores the rights" of the Palestinians. Saudi Arabia announced later that it had decided to place a total embargo on all future oil deliveries to the United States, contrary to the hope of many American officials that King Faisal would show moderation in his pressure campaign against Washington. The subsequent decisions of Kuwait, Bahrain, Dubai and Qatar, added to the earlier one by Abu Dhabi, made the Arab boycott of American markets total.

However, the totality of the measures was questionable from the start. Iraq took the position that it would honor the embargo, but refused to have any part in the production cutbacks; it even increased its output in response to world demand. According to U.S. federal energy chief William Simon, almost 700,000 barrels a day of Arab oil was "leaking" through the embargo. This was apparently partly Iraqi oil going through Caribbean and other refineries. The Arab oil that the United States was importing directly after the embargo went into effect represented only 10 per cent of U.S. consumption, but indirectly as well as directly the United States imported about 17 per cent.[12]

---

[11] *Washington Post*, October 20, 1973.

[12] *Ibid.*, March 14, 1974.

Secretary Kissinger took the position, as early as November 1973, that the United States was determined to be guided not by the pressures of other countries, but by the "American conception of the national interest and of the interest of general peace." At the same time he stated that if pressures continue "unreasonably and indefinitely," the United States would have to consider taking countermeasures.[13] In defending this position, the Secretary argued that U.S. peacemaking efforts were begun before the oil embargo was imposed and insisted, time and again, that these efforts must not be linked to the lifting of the embargo. Yet, he himself seemed to link the two. For example, in a meeting with reporters in December 1973, he repeated the frequently stated position that it was "inappropriate" for the Arab states to continue their embargo against the United States while Washington was making every effort to bring about a peaceful solution in the Middle East. "The United States," he said, "could understand certain actions by certain Arab countries when the United States was supplying military equipment to one side in a war." But now that the United States had made a commitment to bring about a settlement, the embargo was no longer appropriate.[14]

To cite an even clearer example of the linkage between American peacemaking efforts and the lifting of the oil embargo, Kissinger predicted in January 1974 that the Arab oil embargo would be lifted even before Egyptian and Israeli forces completed the projected 40-day disengagement of their forces along the Suez Canal under the first Sinai agreement. "We have every reason to believe," he told reporters, "that success in the negotiations would mark a major step toward ending the oil embargo."[15] Although the Secretary would not say so, it was clear at the time that President Sadat, in close and cordial contact with the Secretary, was trying to persuade other Arab states to lift the embargo. On January 24, 1974, the *Washington Post* commented: "It would be altogether welcome and appropriate if the American-sponsored disengagement accord, as a bonus, produced an end to the embargo." In essence, the Secretary's use of his peace mission for the lifting of the oil embargo was a shrewd move, even if he insisted officially on an artificial separation of the two. By using its peacemaking efforts to get the embargo lifted, the United States, in fact, was trying to take advantage of the Arab policy which sought to pressure Israel through the United States.

The linkage between American peacemaking efforts and the Arab oil embargo was even more evident in the Secretary's strenuous "shuttle diplomacy" to negotiate the Syrian-Israeli disengagement agreement.

---

[13] DOS, News Release, November 21, 1973, pp. 1-12.

[14] *Washington Post*, December 28, 1973.

[15] *Ibid.*, January 23, 1974.

Both Kissinger and Nixon hinted in February 1974 that Sadat was trying to convince Arab oil producers to lift the embargo as a sign of good faith toward the United States, which had played the main role in arranging the Israeli pullback from the West Bank of the Suez Canal, due to be completed by February 21.[16] The Secretary went on his mission in February after Nixon's meeting with Saudi Arabian Foreign Minister Omar Saqqaf and Egyptian Foreign Minister Ismail Fahmi. Behind the drive to get a rapid disengagement on the Golan Heights, according to the *Washington Post*, was the expectation that the Arab states might lift the oil embargo once there was progress on the Syrian front. According to Edward Sheehan, Syria urged a prolongation of the embargo, but Saqqaf and Fahmi told Nixon and Kissinger in effect: "Do something for Syria and the embargo will stop." Kissinger promised to try. In March the embargo was suspended. "Kissinger subsequently denied the 'linkage,' but, in fact, his Syrian shuttle was the price he paid to end the embargo."[17]

It was not a simple undertaking to lift the embargo. Arab "solidarity" was under tremendous strain, a fact that must be remembered in any assessment of a future Arab oil embargo. Without going into a close analysis of the intra-Arab difficulties, it will suffice to recall the Tripoli and Vienna meetings of the Arab oil ministers. They met in Tripoli, Libya, on March 13, 1974, with the expectation of ending the oil embargo against shipments to the United States and restoring production to the pre-October 1973 level. At the time there was speculation that the decision to do so had actually been reached, but its announcement had been postponed in order to avoid embarrassing the Libyans, who opposed the lifting, by announcing such a decision on their soil. However, it became clear later at Vienna that the postponement had been agreed to in the hope of persuading not only Libya, but also Algeria and Syria, to go along with the decision to lift the embargo. When it was finally lifted on March 18, Syria and Libya refused to join the majority and Algeria issued a statement stressing the provisional nature of the agreement which it supported. Although the Arab states refrained from committing themselves to a full restoration of the production cutbacks, they did indicate that output from Arab oilfields would be raised, and the Saudi Arabian Petroleum Minister, Sheikh Zaki Yamani, stated that the United States "can expect to receive at least a million barrels a day" from his country.[18]

More important, the linkage between the embargo and the settlement of the Arab-Israeli conflict was clearly emphasized in Vienna. The formal

---

[16] *Ibid.*, February 14, 1974.
[17] Sheehan, "Step by Step in the Middle East," p. 36.
[18] *Washington Post*, March 15, 18, 19, 1974.

communique issued by the Arab oil ministers at the end of their March 18 meeting stated:

It appeared to the ministers that the American official policy as evidenced greatly by recent political events assumes a new dimension vis-à-vis the Arab-Israeli conflict. Such a dimension, if maintained, will leave Americans to assume a position which is more compatible with the principle of what is right and just toward the Arab occupied territories and the legitimate rights of the Palestinian people.

In justifying the use of oil as a weapon, the communique also stated that the purpose of the ministers has been

to draw the attention of the world to the Arab cause in order to create the suitable political climate for the implementation of United Nations Security Council Resolution 242 which calls for complete withdrawal from the Arab occupied territories and the restoration of the legitimate rights of the Palestinian people.

This was, of course, the Arab interpretation of that resolution, but the more interesting point is that the Arab states' position at this time was quite different from October 17, 1973, when they decided to impose the embargo. As noted before, they had then stated in Kuwait that the cutbacks to the United States and other industrialized countries supporting Israel could continue until Israel withdrew from the Arab lands it occupied in the 1967 war and restored "the rights of the Palestinians." Neither objective had in fact been achieved when the embargo was lifted.

A difficult problem facing American policymakers in the future is whether or not to adopt countermeasures if and when a new embargo is reimposed by Saudi Arabia. This is no hypothetical problem. The need for countermeasures was hinted at in one way or another by American leaders and scholars alike during the period 1973-1975, and this point was unequivocally made by Jimmy Carter when he was the Democratic presidential candidate. In fact, Saudi and American military, political and economic relations have deepened so greatly since the war that deciding on countermeasures might pose a more difficult problem for the United States today. To be sure, some observers believe that the other side of the coin of deeper American stakes in Saudi Arabia is the great dependence of that country on American technology, military equipment and economic and commercial cooperation. These ties, they argue, would act as a "handle" on the Saudis. But such an argument is not satisfactory to those who are, for example, concerned about the possibility of transfer of arms in another war from the Persian Gulf area to the "frontline" Arab states at war with Israel. Furthermore, so long as the possibility of a new war exists, the chances of reimposition of another embargo are real.

Consumer Solidarity

The rhetoric of "global interdependence," "global cooperation," and "cooperation rather than confrontation" aside, the United States pursued two other tactics in response to the Arab oil embargo, in addition to expediting its peacemaking efforts outlined above. These were the threat of countermeasures, and the creation of a common front with Japan and Western Europe as a means of applying pressure against the oil-producing states and of entering into a dialogue with them if the circumstances warranted.

Because the latter tactic relates more to the problems of transatlantic relations, which are beyond the scope of this study, I shall examine it only briefly here in order to show the nature of the American attitude toward the Middle East states and relate this attitude subsequently to the overall problem of the American conception of the area. It was clear from the outset that, in spite of all the rhetoric of cooperation and dialogue, Secretary Kissinger wished to confront the Arab oil-producing states with a united front consisting of Japan, the West European states and the United States. That this was indeed a major objective of the Secretary is evident from policy statements and actions. In the first place, the producer nations were simply excluded from the Washington Conference held in February 1974. In the second place, even after the conference, when Kissinger was asked his view on having representatives from the producing nations sit in with the coordinating group to prepare for the later conference, he stated:

Well, there are two problems, at least, in the work of the coordinating group. One is to analyze and to give impetus to certain types of activities which are enumerated in the communique [of the Washington Conference], such as conservation of energy, a system of allocating oil supplies, acceleration of the development of additional energy resources, acceleration of energy research and development. Also, the need to find financial mechanisms to deal with some of the problems produced by higher prices. That work of the coordination group seems to us to be primarily confined to the countries that participate in this conference and countries with similar problems.[19]

Yet these problems obviously concerned the producer nations as well, particularly considering the Secretary's repeated analysis of these and other energy problems in terms of "global interdependence" and "global cooperation." Furthermore, it was universally recognized that the establishment of the International Energy Agency (IEA) under the auspices of the United States was a device in part to confront the producer nations with the "solidarity" of the consumer nations' position. Thomas O. End-

---

[19] DOS, News Release, February 13, 1974, p. 3.

ers, Assistant Secretary of State, at times could not hide his condescending attitude toward the oil producers. In a statement on IEA, for example, he stated that

all IEA members will benefit by avoiding pressure on price during any future crisis. The provisions for emergency reserves, demand restraint, and sharing of available oil should provide the necessary protection against the chaotic situation and *irrational behavior* of the producer nations which triggered soaring prices during the last embargo.[20]

The Secretary of State's confrontation tactics, in spite of his cooperation rhetoric, were in large part responsible for the failure of the first consumer-producer conference held in Paris in April 1975. Only subsequent to the breakdown of that multilateral meeting did the Secretary propose the "new approach to the launching of a dialogue, broadening it to include the whole range of relations between industrial and developing countries,"[21] that had been demanded by the latter at Paris. "After the collapse last April of a preparatory meeting for a conference between oil producers and consumers," the *New York Times* reported, "the United States changed its position on the scope of the conference."[22]

The Secretary himself admitted, after the collapse of the Paris meeting, that "Our own thinking on the issue of raw materials, and the manner in which it can be addressed internationally, has moved forward";[23] that is, it moved closer to the position of the so-called third world countries. But other Administration officials seemed to be calling practically for a new "cold war" between the "North and South." The most outspoken member of this school of thought, the colorful and controversial Daniel P. Moynihan, published his manifesto, "The United States in Opposition," shortly before the Paris meeting. His diagnosis of the source of the behavior of all developing nations interests us here only because of the discussion below concerning the perceptual traps that complicate our understanding of the Middle East situation. Although acknowledging that these countries vary in size, population and resources, they are, he asserted, in one respect "indistinguishable." They are ideologically uniform because their politics derived from "the general corpus of British socialist opinion as it developed in the period roughly 1890-1950."[24]

---

[20] *Ibid.*, February 1975 (sic), p. 3. (Emphasis added.)

[21] *Ibid.*, July 14, 1975, p. 3.

[22] *New York Times*, August 19, 1975.

[23] Department of State, *The Secretary of State*, May 13, 1975, p. 4.

[24] Daniel P. Moynihan, "The United States in Opposition," *Commentary*, March 1975, pp. 31-44; and his "Presenting the American Case," *The American Scholar*, Autumn 1975, pp. 564-583.

Threats of Countermeasure

In a press conference held on November 21, 1973, Secretary of State Kissinger stated: "However, it is clear that if pressures continue unreasonably and indefinitely, . . . the United States will have to consider what countermeasures it may have to take. We would do this with enormous reluctance and we are still hopeful that matters will not reach this point."[25] Both President Ford and Secretary Kissinger, in their addresses to the UN General Assembly in September 1974, linked the problems of oil and food prices. The President admonished the producers for "production restrictions" and "artificial pricing" and told them that they "will eventually become the victims of their own actions."[26] The Secretary stated that the "present price level even threatens the economic well-being of producers."

Arab delegates to the United Nations regarded President Ford's address to the Assembly as a veiled ultimatum to the oil-producing countries; they believed that the United States was trying to "rally the majority of the world against" the Arabs, and to link the energy and food crises in order to "intimidate" the oil-producing countries.[27] Even Egypt took a militant position in defending Arab oil policies. Alluding to Ford's and Kissinger's addresses, Fahmi, the Egyptian Foreign Minister, declared it was "regrettable" to hear it "even claimed that the fragile framework of international economic cooperation would be exposed to danger if the oil-producing countries continue their present pricing policies."[28] On the same day that Kissinger was addressing the UN General Assembly, President Ford seemed to be linking price increases to war in his speech to the Ninth World Energy Conference. He stated: "When nations use their resources as political weapons against others, the result is human suffering. . . . Throughout history, nations have gone to war over natural advantages such as water or food or convenient passage on land and sea."[29]

The threat of countermeasures, however, was less veiled in the Secretary of State's controversial interview with *Business Week* of January 13, 1975. In response to a question whether he had considered taking military action against the oil price increase, the Secretary replied:

A very dangerous course. We should have learned from Viet-Nam that it is easier to get into a war than to get out of it. I am not saying that there is no circumstance

---

[25] DOS, News Release, November 21, 1973, p. 3.

[26] *Ibid.*, September 23, 1974, Address by President Gerald R. Ford before the 29th Session of the UN General Assembly, September 18, 1974, p. 3; *ibid.*, Address by Secretary of State Henry A. Kissinger before the 29th Session of the UN, September 23, 1974.

[27] See *New York Times*, September 20, 1974.

[28] *Ibid.*, October 2, 1974.

[29] DOS, News Release, September 23, 1974, p. 2.

where we would not use force. But it is one thing to use it in the case of dispute over price, it's another where there is some actual strangulation of the industrialized world.[30]

In an interview with *Bill Moyers' Journal: International Report* a few days later, the Secretary replied to a question on the unfavorable reaction of the Europeans to his *Business Week* interview in these words: "We did not say—and I repeat here—that any of the issues that are now under discussion fall into this category [of strangulation]. There would have to be an overt move of an extremely drastic, dramatic, and aggressive nature before this contingency could ever be considered."[31] In a subsequent press conference he stated that the contingency to which he referred "could arise only if warfare were originated against the United States. I don't foresee this."[32]

Kissinger did not make clear, however, what he meant by "warfare." If the Secretary had in mind a crippling oil embargo against the United States, it would still have been unwise to adopt such a course of action. An important study prepared for the Congress subsequently pointed up the infeasibility of military intervention in the Persian Gulf oilfields. The study concluded that the success of such a course of action would depend largely on whether only slight damage was caused to key installations, and whether the Soviets refrained from armed intervention.

Since neither essential could be assured, military operations to rescue the United States (much less its key allies) from an air-tight OPEC embargo would combine high costs with high risks wherever we focused our efforts. This country would so deplete its strategic reserves that little would be left for contingencies elsewhere. Prospects would be poor, with plights of far-reaching political, economic, social, psychological, and perhaps military consequences the penalty for failure.[33]

A respected scholar who favored military intervention in the Persian Gulf oilfields was Robert W. Tucker.[34] His thesis was first challenged on grounds of logistical feasibility by Arnaud de Borchgrave, Senior Editor of *Newsweek*,[35] and it was also criticized for reasons of economics, principle, and cost and benefit calculations by numerous readers of *Commentary*, where it was published.[36] He was also criticized for underestimating the

---

[30] *Ibid.*, "Business Week Issue of January 13, 1975," p. 4.

[31] Department of State, *The Secretary of State*, Interview, January 16, 1975.

[32] *Ibid.*, Press Conference, January 28, 1975.

[33] *Oil Fields as Military Objectives: A Feasibility Study*, prepared for the Special Subcommittee on Investigations of The Committee on International Relations (Washington: Government Printing Office, 1975), p. xi.

[34] See Robert W. Tucker, "Oil: The Issue of American Intervention," *Commentary*, January 1975, pp. 21-23; and his "Further Reflections on Oil & Force," *ibid.*, March 1975, pp. 45-46.

[35] *Newsweek*, March 31, 1975.

[36] *Commentary*, April 1975, pp. 5-21.

nature and extent of the Soviet reaction. In taking issue with Tucker's thesis, Stanley Hoffmann stated: "Impatience with uncertainty, and the resulting desire to find a radical solution that will save us, and the world, from having to live in uncertainty" is an American trait. "One may understand the longing, without believing that it can ever be fulfilled."[37]

What is of interest here, however, is the puzzling fact that commentators have so far failed to detect the serious dilemma that the linkage between the Persian Gulf and the Arab-Israeli situations poses today for American policymakers engaged in considering countermeasures against Saudi Arabia, the leading Arab oil producer. Under the Guam Doctrine, Saudi Arabia is an "ally" of the United States in the sense that it is one of the pillars of the U.S. "twin pillar" policy in the Persian Gulf, where parallel American, Iranian and Saudi interests in security and stability of the area are entrusted to these two major regional states. Their friendship for the United States is regarded as important, and yet the Saudi oil embargo and Iranian oil price policies have been serious irritants in American relations with these two countries. Neither the slogans of "dialogue" and "partnership"—amid repeated denunciations of the Shah by former U.S. energy chief and Treasury Secretary William Simon—nor the intensity of rapidly expanding American-Iranian and American-Saudi economic cooperation could hide the problems posed by this abiding dilemma. The roots of the dilemma must be sought in conceptual ambiguities in American policy that have surfaced particularly in the period since the October war, during which linkages between the problems of the Persian Gulf and the Arab-Israeli conflict have developed. The problem of the oil embargo, however, forms only one of these linkages. American arms sales is the other major problem that links the Persian Gulf and the Arab-Israeli situations, and it, too, reveals new dilemmas in American policy toward the Middle East.

---

[37] Stanley Hoffmann's letter to the Editor of *Commentary*, April 1975, pp. 5-6.

3.

U.S. Support of the Military Build-Up in the Persian Gulf

E SSENTIAL TO A discussion of the military build-up in the Persian Gulf is a brief review of the policy of the Ford Administration toward this issue. Before the October war, Joseph J. Sisco, Assistant Secretary of State for Near Eastern and South Asian Affairs, attempted to place U.S. arms sales policy in the Persian Gulf in the context of broad American objectives in the area. U.S. objectives were stated to be (1) support for indigenous regional collective security efforts to provide stability and to foster orderly development without outside interference; (2) the peaceful resolution of territorial and other disputes among the regional states; (3) continued access to Persian Gulf oil supplies at reasonable prices and in sufficient amounts to meet "our growing needs and those of our European and Asian friends and allies"; and (4) enhancement of American commercial and financial interests. After the October war, Assistant Secretary Sisco repeated the same general objectives in 1975. In insisting on arms sales as part and parcel of the overall U.S. policy in the Persian Gulf area, Sisco told Lee H. Hamilton, Chairman of the Special Subcommittee on Investigations of the House Committee on International Relations:

Mr. Chairman, I know of the concerns in the Congress and of your personal concerns about our arms supply programs in the Gulf region, and I believe it is important to get these concerns out on the table and discuss them. These are valid questions for Americans, who are troubled at seeing their country in the arms supply business. The image of the "merchant of death" dies hard. I hope I have been able to put this issue into proper and realistic perspective, and to demonstrate that we are dealing with it in the context of an overall and carefully developed policy concept. The fact is that foreign relations are a whole piece. We cannot pick up elements with which we feel comfortable and ignore others. For every country in the world, its ability to defend itself is the most important thing to its national survival. If we do not take this into account in our relations with that country, the totality of our relationship with that country will suffer, as will our political and economic objectives.[38]

---

[38] For Secretary Joseph J. Sisco's statement, see U.S. Congress, House, Committee on Foreign Affairs, *New Perspectives on the Persian Gulf*, Hearings before the Subcommittee on the Near East and South Asia, 93rd Cong., 1st sess. (Washington: Government Printing Office, 1973), pp. 1-10.

Although U.S. arms sales to Iran and Saudi Arabia had been a long-standing policy,[39] they increased in keeping with the twin pillar policy adopted around 1968 when the British announced their decision to withdraw from the Gulf area. But the boom in arms sales has taken place since the explosion of oil prices in 1973. Between 1972 and 1976 arms sales to Iran totalled $10.4 billion, making that country "the largest single purchaser of U.S. military equipment."[40] In 1976 Senator Hubert H. Humphrey published, on behalf of the Subcommittee on Foreign Assistance of the Senate Committee on Foreign Relations, a study of U.S. military sales to Iran, which he promised would be followed by others in a "series of oversight activities in the foreign assistance area."[41] The twelve critical findings of this study, conducted by Robert Mantel and Geoffrey Kemp, range from the problems arising from the sale of large quantities of some of the most sophisticated equipment in the U.S. inventory, to a crucial decision in 1972 by the President to sell Iran "anything it wanted," to socio-economic problems arising out of the presence of large and growing numbers of Americans in Iran. I shall comment on this study later. It will be helpful at this point to categorize in broad terms some of the most important types of criticism that have been directed against U.S. arms sales to the Persian Gulf area.

Arms Sales Debate

One of the major arguments against U.S. arms sales in the Persian Gulf area is the arms race. Some observers regard a Persian Gulf arms race as a definite possibility, while others believe there already is an arms race between Iran and Iraq, or Iran and Saudi Arabia, which is likely to spread to other countries of the area as well. This argument is usually coupled with the fear that the arms race holds potential for armed conflict. Since the area is rich not only in oil but also in territorial, tribal, continental shelf, dynastic, ideological, political, economic and other disputes, massive arms sales might aggravate, it is argued, the already existing conflicts, and even cause new tensions and additional types of conflict.

Another argument against arms sales is based on the fear of American involvement in a conflict-prone and unstable area. According to the Senate staff study, there were some 24,000 Americans resident in Iran alone in 1976 and the number is expected to reach between 50,000 and 60,000 by 1980-1981. The presence of such a large and growing number

---

[39] See *ibid.*, for background on U.S. arms sales to Saudi Arabia; see Rouhollah K. Ramazani, *Iran's Foreign Policy, 1941-1973: A Study of Foreign Policy in Modernizing Nations* (Charlottesville: University Press of Virginia, 1975) on the background of U.S. arms sales to Iran.

[40] *U.S. Military Sales to Iran*, A Staff Report to the Subcommittee on Foreign Assistance of the Committee on Foreign Relations, United States Senate (Washington: Government Printing Office, 1976).

[41] *Ibid.*, p. iii.

of Americans in the Gulf area can give rise to anti-Americanism, and it can also place U.S., citizens in jeopardy as hostages in a Vietnam-like situation.[42]

The relationship between oil and arms sales has been attacked primarily at two levels. At one level, it is argued, the policy of using arms sales as a means of correcting U.S. balance of payments problems, precipitated in part by the escalation of oil prices, is short-sighted in the sense that the benefits are far outweighed by the threat to world peace.[43] At the other level, the Administration's apparent willingness to engage in barter-like arrangements for exchanging arms for oil is criticized because it enables countries, such as Iran, to continue to acquire large quantities of sophisticated weapons. As early as 1969 Iran was interested in such transactions, but the United States proved impervious to Iranian overtures when the Shah visited the United States. During his 1973 visit, however, when American concern with the "energy crisis" was increasing—even before the October war and the oil embargo—the United States seemed far more receptive to the idea; it was the lead item on the agenda of President Nixon's talks with the Shah in Washington. In 1976 the idea was realized in a spectacular manner when Iran and the United States signed a $40 billion trade agreement for the 1976-1980 period, under which Iran will sell oil worth $14 billion to the United States, plus $2 million worth of other goods. According to some critics, about 10 of the 24 billion dollars in projected American sales to Iran are earmarked for arms.[44]

Some critics insist that, contrary to expectations, arms sales to Persian Gulf countries are not likely to secure a balance of power in the area. For example, Robert E. Hunter, Senior Fellow of the Overseas Development Council, states:

In general, I believe that the concept of military balance which is used so often in the world may simply not apply in the region of the Persian Gulf. To have a military balance you need clear lines of confrontation, deterrent capabilities on both sides, command and control of forces, plus an adequate relationship between warning time, intelligence gathering, and a political decision process; otherwise it may not be possible to prevent war by accident. In the Gulf it is rare to find the combination of these necessary factors of military balance. In fact, the introduction of high performance aircraft into an area of short distances and flat terrain can make conflict all the more likely.[45]

A number of critics fear that unlimited sales of sophisticated conventional weapons might whet the appetites of the larger affluent states of the

---

[42] See Edward M. Kennedy, "The Persian Gulf: Arms Race or Arms Control," *Foreign Affairs*, October 1975, pp. 14-35; and *U.S. Military Sales to Iran*.

[43] See the *Washington Post*, January 27, 1976.

[44] *Christian Science Monitor*, August 17, 1976.

[45] *New Perspectives on the Persian Gulf*, p. 73.

Persian Gulf for nuclear weapons. The Indian nuclear explosion, for example, might already have increased the Shah's desire to "go nuclear," in spite of his repeated assertions that Iran's current interest in nuclear energy is only for peaceful purposes. There is little doubt that the Indian explosion of a nuclear device had a profound impact on Iran's interest in acquiring nuclear reactors from France, Germany and the United States. There is also little doubt that the diversion of nuclear energy to nuclear explosives is technologically not difficult.

Finally, the vast and costly arms purchases by developing nations are considered detrimental to their social systems. The Iranian government has repeatedly denied that this is the case, because it can afford both "butter and guns" and, therefore, its arms build-up is not necessarily at the expense of socio-economic development. One student of the Iranian domestic scene, however, has argued vigorously that American arms sales policies are bound to affect adversely the long-range interests of both the United States and Iran. Marvin Zonis' testimony was characterized by Lee H. Hamilton, Chairman of the House Subcommittee on the Near East and South Asia, as a "devastating indictment" of Iranian policies. According to Hamilton, Zonis charged that corruption was pervasive, torture had become an accepted instrument of regime policy, the secret police permeated the society, terrorism and assassination were rampant, economic growth benefited only the upper strata, and the government was not interested in the wide dissemination of wealth. Furthermore, the regime projected an increasingly aggressive Iranian posture throughout the area.[46]

A Critique of the Arms Sales Debate

In the light of our primary concern with conceptual problems involved in American policy in the Middle East, it is interesting to note that both the defenders and critics of American arms sales tend to avoid addressing the fundamental conceptual problems involved. For example, there is no evidence that the Nixon and Ford administrations, in defending their positions, had been aware of the conceptual ambiguity underlying overall policies. The same is true of the Carter Administration, despite its new arms sales policy.

I am inclined to think that conceptual ambiguity still lies at the heart of the arms sales policy. For example, former Assistant Secretary of State Sisco's claim, in the statement quoted previously, that the United States is dealing with the arms sales issue "in the context of an overall and carefully developed policy concept" hangs in the air, since he makes no serious

---

[46] *Ibid.*, p. 91.

attempt to indicate what that "policy concept" is. Obviously, listing the general objectives of U.S. policy in the Persian Gulf can hardly be viewed as a substitute for such a concept. Nor is it sufficient to imply that the United States regards Iran and Saudi Arabia as the "key" countries of the Gulf area for maintaining security and stability in keeping with the Guam Doctrine. The Carter Administration has not yet related its new arms sales principles to its overall "new foreign policy." Neither Iran nor Saudi Arabia can really know what the new U.S. Persian Gulf policy is today.

This "twin pillar" concept raises more questions than it answers. If support of the "collective security" efforts of the Persian Gulf states is still our number one objective—and it is so listed—then it must be asked how "collective" is that concept. The pragmatic argument that, when the twin-pillar idea first surfaced, Iraq, for example, could not possibly have been regarded as a contributor to Persian Gulf collective security because it was "anti-Western" raises still another question. How does this basically cold war conception of the Persian Gulf states fit in with the Guam Doctrine, which calls for replacing "the impulses of the previous cold war era" and asserts, as one of its basic tenets, that "other nations can and should assume greater responsibilities, for their sake as well as ours." Does the Guam Doctrine mean the continuation of the cold war between the United States and the Soviet Union by proxy (between Iran and Iraq, for example), or does it mean U.S. support for *any* regional power capable of contributing to regional order? If the latter is the case, the re-establishment of U.S. diplomatic relations with Iraq must be given a higher priority by the new Administration.

These persistent conceptual ambiguities also lay at the root of most criticism directed against the previous Administration's arms sales in the Persian Gulf. Some critics still assume that the cold war is quiescent, if not totally dead, and are hence inclined to question not only our own concern with the Soviet Union, but also the apprehensions of arms recipient countries about Soviet intentions and policies in the Persian Gulf area. This is not a wholly warranted assumption. It is difficult to conclude that Soviet-American detente has been successful in the Gulf area or in the Arab-Israeli zone of the Middle East. The problem of Soviet and communist support of subversion and insurrection—as in Oman, directly as well as through Iraq, South Yemen and Cuba in the past—is today a source of legitimate concern about the future. And the effectiveness of detente in the Arab-Israeli conflict is at least open to question.[47] Some critics also want to have their cake and eat it, too. They seem to welcome tacitly the

---

[47] On detente and the Arab-Israeli conflict of 1973, see Foy D. Kohler, Leon Gouré and Mose L. Harvey, *The Soviet Union and the October Middle East War: The Implications for Detente* (Coral Gables, Fla.: Center for Advanced International Studies, University of Miami, Monographs in International Affairs, 1974). On detente and the Persian Gulf area, see Ramazani, pp. 355-369, 395-438.

tenets of the Guam Doctrine, that is, the United States should not police the world; regional powers should have the primary responsibility for regional security; and it is better to sell arms than commit American troops abroad. But at the same time, they decry American arms sales abroad on moral, social, economic and political grounds.

A number of moderate critics, who were dissatisfied with the previous practice of arms sales, suggested that the United States should follow several new guidelines in formulating an arms sales policy. The best example of this approach was reflected in a special study conducted by Congressman Pierre S. DuPont IV, a member of the House Committee on International Relations, in Iran, Kuwait and Saudi Arabia from May 22 to 31, 1975, and published in January 1976.[48] Convinced that an "effective U.S. military presence in the Gulf is difficult and expensive to operate," while U.S. interests increasingly involved insuring American access to oil supplies and trade avenues, the author called on the United States to define "its own legitimate concerns in the area of the Persian Gulf and decide whether or not the arms buildup" of the three countries mentioned above and other future purchases of U.S. arms was in the U.S. national interest. Rather than a direct U.S. military presence in the Gulf, the study suggested, the United States "can secure its interests by providing nations friendly to the United States with the military capability to protect the area from outside interference and to insure its stability." Toward this end, however, the United States should (1) avoid heavy injection of armaments into the Persian Gulf; (2) not contribute to a regional arms race; (3) estimate the likelihood of arms transfers from recipient countries to other Middle East countries; (4) set limits on the levels of sophistication of the arms it is prepared to sell; (5) weigh the advantages and disadvantages of coproduction; and (6) define what its training and equipping of a foreign nation means in terms of a U.S. commitment to that nation.

The more recent study, *U.S. Military Sales to Iran*, conducted by Mantel and Kemp, argues that the "normal" arms transfer review processes in the United States were bypassed in the sales of sophisticated arms to Iran because President Nixon decided in 1972 to sell Iran "anything it wanted." The study infers that the President's decision was based upon "broad geostrategic and political considerations" without making any attempt to spell these out. In my opinion, the single most important consideration was to assuage the Shah's fears about the possible adverse implications of detente for Iran's relations with the United States. The President tried to assure the Shah in Tehran on his way back from the Moscow summit that the United States and the Soviet Union had no

---

[48] See *United States Arms Sales to the Persian Gulf*, Report of a Study Mission to Iran, Kuwait, and Saudi Arabia, May 22-31, 1975 (Washington: Government Printing Office, 1975).

intention of imposing a condominium on the world, that the United States remained an ally of Iran, and that the United States would continue to support Iran's military build-up for carrying out new responsibilities in the Persian Gulf area.[49] In light of these assurances, it is reasonable to suggest that the President's decision was a price paid in the pursuit of detente. This decision also points up the still unresolved problem of defining (1) U.S. objectives in the Persian Gulf area, (2) the relationships among the concepts of detente, the Guam Doctrine, and the containment of the Soviet Union, and (3) the impact of these concepts upon American policy in the Persian Gulf.

The Persian Gulf Military Build-Up and the Arab-Israeli Conflict

Conceptual ambiguity, if not confusion, about U.S. arms sales in the Persian Gulf creates dilemmas in American policy extending beyond that area. The dilemma is only in part how to formulate an arms sales policy in the Gulf without jeopardizing the security and stability of the countries of the area. More urgent problems arise out of the "military build-up" linkage between the Persian Gulf situation and the Arab-Israeli conflict. The concept of "military build-up" is used here rather than the usual notion of "arms transfer" because it is broader; it includes arms transfer problems but is not limited to these. One aspect of the linkage is the arms transfer from the Gulf states to the "confrontation" states. The proponents of arms sales argue that the U.S. Foreign Military Sales Act prohibits the unauthorized transfer of arms to third countries and obligates the United States to terminate all military sales to the offending nation:

. . . any foreign country which hereafter uses defense articles or defense services, such country under this Act, in substantial violation of any provision of this Act, shall be immediately ineligible for further cash sales, credits, or guarantees.[50]

Defenders of arms sales also contend that one cannot assume that equipment sold by the United States, for example, to Saudi Arabia or Kuwait, will find its way into the hands of one of the combatants in any new war in the Middle East. They base this conclusion primarily on two factors: (1) the relationship of the equipment to the defense needs of recipient countries; and (2) the heavy dependence of the recipients on continued U.S. support. The first factor is important because both the United States and recipient countries understand that the weapons purchased from the United States are for the recipients' own defenses, and

---

[49] See Ramazani, p. 369-371.
[50] *United States Arms Sales to the Persian Gulf*, p. 22.

not for stockpiling or diversion to other Arab nations. The second factor deters because the weapons that might be used in a new war—such as aircraft, anti-aircraft missiles, antitank weapons and artillery—are now, and will be for some years to come, heavily dependent on continued U.S.-supplied spare parts, training, maintenance and other support, and Washington can exert control over unauthorized transfers of these weapons by withdrawing support. Since the recipients understand that this will happen, they will refrain from transferring them.[51]

Others believe, however, that neither the Act nor the factors mentioned provide a guarantee against arms transfers; there is, in fact, no foolproof guarantee against arms transfers. The best safeguard, they argue, is a prudent selection of U.S. arms recipients. For example, according to this thesis, Kuwait would probably not be a prudent choice, since it would have a difficult time resisting the pressure of its large Palestinian population to transfer arms to the preferred combatants in a Middle East conflict.[52]

Another problem arises from the fact that there is no legal obstacle in the way of a country, equipped with American arms, to come to the aid of a third nation. For example, non-Arab Iran, during the 1973 Arab-Israeli war, transported Saudi troops to Syria in U.S.-supplied C-130 aircraft, although it ceased the practice upon delivery of an American protest. The only leverage the United States has in such an instance is to express disapproval and hope for the best.[53]

In considering the linkage of the Persian Gulf military build-up and the Arab-Israeli conflict, another issue that must be examined is coproduction. At the moment, Iran is anxious to become self-sufficient in various aspects of its military build-up. The United States has already given approval in principle to a small number of coproduction proposals, including manufacturing in Iran of a utility-type helicopter and a couple of missile systems—the TOW and Maverick.[54] There is no reason to believe that Saudi Arabia would not be interested in some kind of coproduction agreement in the future. Although the transfer of weapons manufactured under license is subject to the same nontransfer restrictions as the transfer of weapons produced in the United States, the end use of the arms so manufactured would be more difficult to ascertain and control.[55] Another aspect of the coproduction problem is what may be called "proxy coproduction." So far this problem has not gained much

---

[51] See U.S. Congress, House, Committee on International Relations, *The Persian Gulf, 1975: The Continuing Debate on Arms Sales*, Hearings before the Special Subcommittee on Investigations, 94th Cong., 1st sess. (Washington: Government Printing Office, 1975), p. 69.

[52] See *United States Arms Sales to the Persian Gulf*, p. 23.

[53] *Ibid.*, p. 24.

[54] See *The Persian Gulf, 1975: The Continuing Debate on Arms Sales*, p. 68.

[55] See *United States Arms Sales to the Persian Gulf*, p. 24.

attention, but if it is true that Iran and Egypt are discussing a joint arms producing industry then the matter is worth watching.[56]

There are several other aspects of the linkage between the Persian Gulf military build-up and the Arab-Israeli conflict that bear watching. Huge reserves of petrodollars make it possible for the Gulf states to fund weapons procurement by "confrontation" states. The financing of Egyptian, Syrian and Jordanian military purchases is already going on. The fact that the bulk of the sophisticated weapons that Egypt has purchased since the October War with Persian Gulf money consists of weapons of British and French origin—and in the case of Syria, weapons of Soviet origin—does not alter the basic problems of arms balance and arms control.

Besides funding, the training function is an increasing problem in the linkage between the Persian Gulf military build-up and the Arab-Israeli conflict. For example, Egypt's "back door" policy is reportedly designed to purchase arms through other countries if its needs are not met by direct purchases from the United States. According to Egyptian sources, this policy could also apply to the training of Egyptian servicemen in the use of U.S. equipment.[57] Iran, the single largest purchaser of American arms, is trying to forge some sort of defense cooperation agreement with Egypt in light of the growing Soviet military presence in the Indian Ocean, the Red Sea and the Gulf of Aden. The implications of this kind of military cooperation would seem to be difficult to confine only to the areas of common Iranian-Egyptian concern. Reportedly, "senior Egyptian air force officers" have flown in the F-4 fighter bombers sold by the United States to Iran.[58]

Conceptual Ambiguities

The increasing linkages between the Persian Gulf military build-up and the Arab-Israeli conflict, even more than the probability of a new oil embargo, pose new dilemmas in American policy toward the Middle East. The United States is committed to the survival and security of Israel. At the same time it has become the largest single supplier of arms to Saudi Arabia and an increasingly important supplier to other "conservative" Arab states of the Persian Gulf under the Guam Doctrine. There is little doubt that this policy has caused concern in Israel, and is cited by Israelis as a reason for expecting even greater U.S. arms aid to their nation.[59] It may be argued that the attitude of the Saudi leadership toward Israel has

---

[56] *Washington Post*, June 18, 1976.

[57] *Ibid.*

[58] *Ibid.*, November 23, 1975.

[59] See *The Persian Gulf, 1975: The Continuing Debate on Arms Sales*, pp. 256-261.

undergone a change in recent years. For example, in his first exclusive interview in 1970 with Arnaud de Borchgrave of *Newsweek*, King Faisal made it clear that he did not subscribe to the 1967 UN resolution, in contrast to Egypt and Jordan, as the basis for the settlement of the Arab-Israeli conflict. Although the King acknowledged the "right to exist" for Israel, he added, "but not as a purely Jewish state. Palestinians must be given the option of returning to their homeland where they must have equal rights with the Jewish cousins. Then we will see the beginning of real peace."[60]

Subsequent indications that Saudi Arabia's position on Israel might have softened, such as King Khalid's attitude toward Jerusalem,[61] do not seem convincing to the Israelis. For example, as late as October 1976, Yigal Allon, then Israeli Foreign Minister, although admitting that "not all the Arab states are cut from the same cloth," stressed that "the Arab states seek to isolate, strangle and erase Israel from the world's map."[62] Certainly Allon is no Israeli "hawk," nor is his perception of Arab intentions regarding Israel an exception. I talked to Israelis in all walks of life in late 1974 and early 1975 and believe that this perception is widely shared in Israel today, although there are others who perceive Arab intentions quite differently. It is difficult to believe that such Israeli perceptions of Arab intentions will soften as a result of the Likud Party's assumption of power.

Obviously, campaign rhetoric should not be taken too seriously, but the views of the 1976 Democratic presidential candidate should be carefully noted, especially now that he is the President. In regard to arms shipments to Israel, as contrasted with Arab states, Carter's position is symptomatic of the dilemma of how to reconcile our new "special relationship" with Saudi Arabia—the largest Arab recipient of American weapons—under the Guam Doctrine, with our older "special relationship" with Israel. Before the October War, the United States refused to entertain the idea of establishing a "special relationship" wtih Saudi Arabia, as evidenced by its negative attitude toward the Saudi proposal for an agreement on the flow of oil supplies to the United States.[63] But it is widely accepted that the set of agreements the United States signed with Saudi Arabia in June 1974 has established a "special relationship" amounting to an "informal economic and military alliance" between the two countries. As seen from Washington, this new relationship provides the inducement

---

[60] For the text of the interview, see *Newsweek*, December 21, 1970, p. 43.

[61] *New York Times*, April 3, 1975.

[62] Yigal Allon, "Israel: The Case for Defensible Borders," *Foreign Affairs*, October 1976, p. 38.

[63] For the text of Shaykh Ahmad Zaki Yamani's address, see the Middle East Institute, *World Energy Demands and the Middle East*, Part I, 26th Annual Conference, Washington, D.C., September 29-30, 1972, pp. 95-100.

for expansion of Saudi oil production, while the Saudis emphasize that the long-range development of good U.S.-Arab relations is contingent on further Israeli withdrawals from Arab lands and "the recognition of Palestinian national rights."[64]

According to Jimmy Carter, "under the last Democratic administration 60% of all weapons that went into the Middle East were for Israel. Now 60% goes to Arab countries and this does not include Iran. If you include Iran in our present shipment of weapons to the Middle East, only 20 per cent goes to Israel."[65] The Democratic presidential candidate went on to observe: "This is a deviation from idealism; it is a deviation from a commitment to our major ally in the Middle East which is Israel."

The charge that this and similar campaign statements were really aimed at winning the Jewish vote is not a revelation, but from the perspective of this study Carter's statements demonstrate anew that linkages between the military build-up in the Persian Gulf and the Arab-Israeli confrontation do pose a dilemma for American policymakers: how to reconcile our "special relationships" with two states locked in bitter conflict. This dilemma, as well as that of how to counter effectively another oil embargo by our "ally," Saudi Arabia, seem to have their roots in the same conceptual problems. Since the October War, we have tended to respond to the pressure of extremely complex and fast-moving events without adequate consideration of conceptual problems inherent in our various policies. The impression that our activities tend to be largely pragmatic, *ad hoc*, uncoordinated and incoherent is not wholly unjustified.

Regardless of the issue, we seem to continue to perceive the Middle East in terms of segments of separate problems arising out of two self-contained situations, one in the Gulf area, and the other in the Arab-Israeli zone. Yet, the linkages that have in fact developed among the problems facing American policymakers since the October War defy such a dual conception. Furthermore, our schizophrenic tendencies are reflected not only with regard to our perceptions of the Middle East situation and a division between the issues of the Gulf area and the Arab-Israeli zone, but also with regard to the cold war and detente, and the cold war and the Guam Doctrine, and we have never bothered to examine the interrelationship of these concepts and their relevance to our overall Middle East policy. Some observers used to charge that we had no Middle East policy, only an "Israeli policy." Edward Sheehan contends that now we do have "an Arab policy,"[66] as a result of Secretary Kissinger's shuttle diplomacy.

---

[64] *Washington Post*, June 8, 9, 1974.

[65] See the text of the transcript of the Ford-Carter debate in the *New York Times*, October 8, 1976.

[66] Sheehan defines the U.S. "Arab policy" by stating that its "essence was a commitment to the Arabs that, so long as they understood the United States would not abandon Israel, Washington would truly wield its power to regain Arab rights." See his "Step by Step in the Middle East," p. 17.

If so, how do these policies relate to the various concepts identified above? So long as American policy does not seem to relate to a comprehensive and coherent conceptual framework, we are apt to continue muddling through old problems and inadvertently creating new ones, as we go along.

4.
Foreign Policy in the Middle East

Looking From the Inside Out

IN TRYING TO formulate a comprehensive and coherent conception of American policy in the Middle East, we must not only overcome the conceptual ambiguities and confusions outlined above, but also avoid the official and unofficial attitudes that have been revealed in our policy statements and courses of action since the October War. As already noted, Secretary Kissinger charged "blackmail," made veiled threats of military intervention, actually linked his peacemaking efforts to the lifting of the oil embargo (despite his claim of no linkage), excluded the oil producers from the Washington Conference, and attempted to confront the oil producers with a united front of consumers (despite the rhetoric of "interdependence," "dialogue" and "cooperation"), while his assistant, Thomas O. Enders, was calling the producers' policies "irrational" and President Ford was hinting at a food embargo as a countermeasure against the Arab states. The Democratic presidential candidate in 1976 also stated unequivocally that he would consider another Arab oil embargo as an "economic declaration of war" and would respond "instantly and in kind." These are the kinds of extreme attitudes of U.S. policymakers that should go unexpressed in the future.

Unofficial American attitudes toward Middle East societies are not on the whole greatly dissimilar from the official ones, although exceptions may be found. As already noted, Robert Tucker favored military intervention in the Persian Gulf oilfields, Daniel Moynihan found the United States in opposition to the whole third world at the height of the energy crisis, and Marvin Zonis launched an "indictment" against the Shah's regime on every conceivable ground. In turn, Stanley Hoffmann considered Tucker's advocacy of military intervention in the Persian Gulf oilfields to be a reflection of a traditional American trait, namely, impatience with uncertainty. This may well be the case, but I believe the problem is more a matter of our attitude toward Middle East societies and culture.

The basic attitudinal problem is that we tend to view the Middle East largely from the outside. This is obviously necessary, but it is not sufficient in the sense that an adequate and sensitive estimate of the Middle East situation requires an ability to view the situation from the inside out as well. This points up the need for what I call an "empirical empathic" approach as another prerequisite for formulating a comprehensive, coherent, and realistic conception of the Middle East. In chapters two and three, I pointed out the conceptual ambiguities in U.S. policy toward the Middle East by examining the region from the vantage point of American policymakers. That is, I tried to look at the environment of U.S. policy from the outside. In this chapter I shall attempt to look at the Middle East from the inside outward, while still bearing in mind the concerns of American policymakers.

One major point needs emphasis before we proceed further. The view of "empirical empathy" rejects the simple notion that U.S. policymakers would be better off, in formulating policy toward the Middle East, if they would take into consideration Middle East perceptions. These perceptions are important, but they alone are not decisive for a better understanding of the Middle East. Understanding Middle East societies in historical as well as modern times requires taking serious note of (a) the *realities* of the situation or circumstances faced by Middle East policymakers as well as their *perceptions* of these realities, and (b) the incessant tension between the two as it affects the formulation of domestic and foreign policies. Whether this fundamental tension manifests itself between ideal and reality, goal and capability, or theory and practice, one must be aware of it in order to gain a deeper understanding of the domestic and foreign policies of all Middle East societies. Historically, for example, the divergence between the ideal of the Caliph as the guardian of Islamic law and the reality of individuals or groups as absolute rulers, or the discrepancy between the Muslim conception of the international system as two permanently irreconcilable hostile camps of Muslim and non-Muslim worlds and the reality of coexistence between the two are principal examples of this all-pervading tension.

We shall take up this point again, but let us first see how misunderstanding of contemporary Middle East societies may result from overemphasizing the role of, for example, ideology to the exclusion of actual circumstances, or from imposing our own culture-bound frameworks of analysis on non-Western societies such as those of Islam. To illustrate these points, let us take up the perspectives of Moynihan and Zonis, mentioned previously. Application of Moynihan's thesis to Egypt, for example, is of little, if any, help in understanding that country's economic policies. His key to the understanding of third world societies in terms of socialist ideology is juxtaposed against his own ideology of "liberty." It would be tempting to look at President Nasser's "Arab socialism" and conclude that Moynihan is right to state that the third world countries are guided by "the general corpus of British socialist opinion," but then how would he explain President Sadat's so-called open door, or capitalist-oriented, policy of today? Yet in light of Egypt's actual experience, Nasser's so-called socialism of yesterday as well as Sadat's alleged capitalism of today are guided more by the interplay of complicated internal and external practical considerations with ideas than by any fixed modern ideology.

A similar problem exists in Zonis' approach to the Iranian situation. One can easily see the merits of many of his criticisms, but the "indictment" of the Shah's regime, as Congressman Hamilton put it, flows naturally from the kind of assumptions that dictate his approach. The regime's domestic and foreign policies could not be evaluated as "correct" by any analyst when they are measured rigidly against the democratic-liberal yardstick. Iranian behavior, once torn away from its most relevant historical, cultural, economic, political and psychological contexts, can lead to no other conclusion than that, if only the Shah were more liberal, things would be better for Iran both domestically and internationally.

But is this the social scientific approach to the study of developing societies? The most fundamental criticism of "traditional" political science has been its West European and North American bias. "Modern" political science is presumably trying to break away from the old impulses of ethnocentricity. As I will try to show in later sections, "revolutionary" Egypt and "reactionary" Iran face formidable internal and external problems to which they respond in a remarkably similar manner, in spite of past and present differences in leadership. The problems of political participation and welfare in Iran and other developing societies must be viewed in the context of their geographic location and overall experience. Certainly there is room for improvement in all these societies in light of their own values as well as those of the West that they have presumably adopted. But it would be presumptuous for us to think that intolerant attitudes on our part would encourage them to emulate our standards, no matter how desirable we believe them to be. So long as intolerance marks our attitudes toward these societies, we are open to charges of cultural imperialism.

The Broader Context

Essential to an empirical empathic view of the Middle East is an understanding of the major characteristics of modernization in our time. In an assessment of the "modern era," Cyril E. Black identifies five characteristics common to all societies: these include the processes of modernization in the intellectual, political, social, economic and psychological realms.[67] The greatest number of Middle East societies are "late modernizing" ones, and one of the most important characteristics of these societies is the

---

[67] Cyril E. Black, "Challenges to an Evolving Legal Order," in Richard A. Falk and Cyril E. Black, editors, *The Future of the International Legal Order: Vol. 1, Trends and Patterns* (Princeton, N.J: Princeton University Press, 1969), pp. 3-31.

process of national awakening. Even those social scientists who would envisage a world of increasing interdependence acknowledge the pervasive force of modern nationalism in late modernizing societies today. Karl Deutsch, for example, states emphatically that *"not before the vast poverty of Asia and Africa will have been reduced substantially by industrialization, and by gains in living standards and in education—not before then will the age of nationalism and national diversity see the beginning of its end."*[68]

Besides nationalism, these societies are also characterized by economic underdevelopment, though some are developing more rapidly than others; historical and cultural experiences quite different from those of Europe, Russia and North America; and recent attainment of formal political independence, though some nations, such as Egypt and Iran, enjoyed nominal independence for a long time and are heirs to ancient civilizations. Most of the Arab states, however, emerged following the disintegration of the Ottoman Empire after World War I and were subjected then to various forms of Western imperial control, while Israel began its independent statehood only in 1948. The process of attaining statehood in the Arab Middle East finally was concluded in 1967 with the independence of Aden, and in 1971 with the independence of the sheikhdoms located in the lower part of the Persian Gulf, following the British withdrawal.

The processes of national awakening in the Middle East as in the rest of Asia and Africa, however, have not always been sympathetically viewed in the West. E. H. Carr views these processes as nothing else but "a progressive development in the perspective of world history," but what "disturbs and alarms" him

is not the march of progress in Asia and Africa, but the tendency of dominant groups in this country (Britain)—and perhaps elsewhere—to turn a blind or uncomprehending eye on these developments, to adopt towards them an attitude oscillating between mistrustful disdain and affable condescension, and to sink back into paralyzing nostalgia for the past.[69]

It is fascinating to note how applicable Carr's characterization of the British attitudes of the 1950s is to the American attitudes of the 1970s outlined above. The British could blame such condescending and uncomprehending attitudes on the part of their policymakers (such as Anthony Eden's attitude toward Egypt in the Suez crisis) on a legacy of British "colonial mentality," but how can one explain the attitudes of such American officials as Thomas O. Enders, William Simon, and even Henry

---

[68] Karl W. Deutsch, *Nationalism and Social Communication* (Cambridge, Mass.: MIT Press, 1953), p. 165. (Italics in the original.)

[69] E. H. Carr, *What is History?* (Harmondsworth, England: Penguin Books Ltd., 1964), p. 148.

Kissinger, toward the Arab and Iranian oil policies? Thomas C. Barger states that most "Americans including some politicians, diplomats, and economists who should have known better, were unaware that the Arab oil embargo of 1973 was the third imposed by the Arabs . . .,"[70] and George Lenczowski tells us that "as early as 1947, the states of the Arab League decided, at their meeting in Syria, "to use oil as a weapon in the forthcoming struggle over the future of Palestine."[71] The entire history of Middle East oil policies has been inextricably interwoven with the struggle for independence and the processes of nation-building. Yet the demand for participation in and nationalization of the oil-producing facilities, as well as the use of oil as an instrument of foreign policy, have seldom been viewed in the broader context of the national awakening of these societies and their quest for control of their destinies.

As a matter of fact, no foreign or domestic decision of Middle East rulers and elites can be understood outside the context of their cultural and national resurgence. "History cannot be written," states Carr, "unless the historian can achieve some kind of contact with the mind of those about whom he is writing."[72] Similarly, the actions of Middle East leaders cannot be appreciated by American policymakers, or others for that matter, unless such empathy is attained. No intelligence estimate of the Middle East situation will prove adequate for plotting an American policy toward the Middle East, unless, besides knowing our own values, purposes, interests and objectives, we can learn to place ourselves in the shoes of the region's leaders as well. Any analysis of the Middle East is bound to be greatly off the mark so long as we continue to forget that the foreign policy behavior of Middle East rulers and elites cannot be separated from the multifaceted challenges facing their old and new civilizations, whether Muslim or Jewish. The unsympathetic, if not condescending, attitudes that obstruct better understanding of Middle East problems are, in the last analysis, a problem of Western civilization. Wilfred Cantwell Smith's final words in this respect are as applicable today as they were in 1957 when first written in a sympathetic and objective analysis of the Muslim world in modern history. The fundamental weakness of both Western civilization and Christianity, in the modern world, he wrote,

is their inability to recognize that they share the planet not with inferiors but with equals. Unless Western civilization intellectually and socially, politically and economically, and the Christian church theologically, can learn to treat other men

---

[70] Thomas C. Barger, *Energy Policies of the World: Arab States of the Persian Gulf* (Newark, Delaware: Center for the Study of Marine Policy, 1975), p. 39.

[71] George Lenczowski, *Middle East Oil in a Revolutionary Age* (Washington, D.C.: American Enterprise Institute for Public Policy, 1976), p. 4.

[72] Carr, p. 24.

with fundamental respect, these two in their turn will have failed to come to terms with the actualities of the twentieth century. . . . all men today, Muslim or Christian, Oriental or Western, face questions that, though differing in form, are essentially comparable: the deepest questions for all of us today are those that involve us with each other.[73]

Being sympathetic and objective toward the Middle East does not necessarily mean that American policymakers or ourselves as analysts should approve of the behavior of Middle East leaders, whether President Assad, President Sadat, King Khalid, Sultan Qabus, or the Shah of Iran. But it does mean the adoption of a more tolerant, compassionate and respectful attitude toward these societies in the pursuit of our own interests. We may in the long run succeed more in seeking changes in their attitudes and policies by proving more sensitive to their formidable difficulties than by insulting their sensibilities.

Centrality of Rulers

One of the most salient characteristics of Middle East societies is the centrality of rulership. Rulership takes many forms in the area. It may reside in a king as in Iran and Saudi Arabia, in a president as in Egypt and Syria, or in a sheikh as in Bahrain, Kuwait, Oman, Qatar, and the seven sheikhdoms of the Union of Arab Emirates (UAE). The fact that the king in Saudi Arabia is at the head of the royal family and the Shah in Iran is at the helm of a political elite; or that the individual sheikhs, such as Sheikh 'Isa bin Sulman al-Khalifa of Bahrain or Sheikh Sabah al-Salim al-Sabah of Kuwait, are the heads of the ruling families, and these and other ruling families in the Persian Gulf have tribal ancestry; or that the real rulers of Egypt and Syria are called president while that of Iraq is called vice-chairman of the Revolutionary Command Council; or that most of the states have constitutions and many of these seem to subscribe to "democracy" and, except for Iran, most of these constitutions proclaim that these states form part of the larger "Arab Nation"—all these facts are empirically much less significant than the reality that most often domestic and foreign policy decisions are made in these societies by one man or a few men who actually wield the greatest power.

The doctrine of the *umma*, the Community of Muslims, lies at the heart of "all Islamic political concepts,"[74] and the head of the community is Allah and Allah alone. From this central concept in classical Islamic

---

[73] Wilfred Cantwell Smith, *Islam in Modern History* (Princeton, N.J.: Princeton University Press, 1957), p. 350.

[74] See Sir Hamilton Gibb, "Constitutional Organization: The Muslim Community and the State," in Majid Khadduri and Herbert J. Liebesny, editors, *Law in the Middle East* (Washington, D.C.: The Middle East Institute, 1955), p. 3.

political thought followed all other major concepts of "state," "nation," "law" and "government." The concept of "law" ($hariah) in Islam is dissimilar to any Western concepts of law, whether we look at it from the natural law, positive law or canon law, or from the sociological-historical perspective, since Islamic law is regarded as Allah's own command. Both state and government exist for the sole purpose of maintaining and enforcing the law, and the ruler (Caliph) is the guardian of the law. The Muslim concept of the international system, as all other political concepts of Islam, is based on the doctrine of the *umma*. The international system consists of two poles—the house of Islam (*dar al-Islam*) and the house of war (*dar al-harb*). The *umma* resides in the former and is ruled by the caliph, and the unconquered infidels reside in the latter. Between the two worlds there can be no lasting peace, and a state of permanent war prevails.[75] But, as mentioned before, in actuality the two worlds have come to coexist.

The Islamic concept of rulership, however, was penetrated by the older concept of rulership that had prevailed in Iran long before the advent of Islam. The Persian tradition taught the divine right of kings, a doctrine that entered Islamic thought in "its most absolute form, subject only to open religious apostasy on his part . . . it fostered the belief that rebellion was the most heinous of crimes, and its doctrine came to be consecrated in the juristic maxim, 'Sixty years of tyranny are better than an hour of civil strife.' "[76] The transformation of rulership in Islam from classical caliphate to "royal authority" went through three historical stages, according to Ibn Khaldun (died in 1406), the greatest of Islamic political thinkers. The caliphate at first existed "without royal authority," then it became mixed up and confused and finally "royal authority came to exist alone."[77] Once the form of government came to be "royal authority pure and simple," superiority of the ruler "attained the limits of its nature and was employed for particular (worthless) purposes, such as the use of force and the arbitrary gratification of desires and for pleasure."[78]

Not a few of the contemporary analysts of Middle East societies distinguish between the "old" and the "new" rulers on the basis of their social class. One result of such an approach is to spread the notion that old rulers are not really interested in, or capable of, meeting the economic, political, moral, intellectual and psychological challenges of the modern age. The

---

[75] See Majid Khadduri, *War and Peace in the Law of Islam* (Baltimore, Md.: Johns Hopkins University Press, 1955), and his *Islamic Law of Nations: Shaybani's Siyar* (Baltimore: Johns Hopkins University Press, 1966).

[76] See Gibb, *op cit.*, p. 15.

[77] See Ibn Khaldun, *The Muqaddimah: An Introduction to History*, translated from the Arabic by Franz Rosenthal, edited and abridged by N. J. Dawood (London: Routledge and Kegal Paul, 1967), p. 166.

[78] *Ibid.*

new rulers will bring more fundamental transformation to their societies because "they are not deterred by interests of their own from embracing fundamental reforms to improve the daily life of the majority." The reason for this, as Manfred Halpern sees it, for example, is that the new rulers, unlike the old ones, do not define the interest of their societies in terms of "the web of personal loyalties."[79]

Following Halpern's path, James Bill's application of this approach to rulership in Egypt, as contrasted with that in Iran and Saudi Arabia, leads him to the obvious conclusion that President Nasser's reform measures were genuinely fundamental while those of the Shah were less so. As we shall see, however, these distinctions are not borne out by the facts. Judged by the actual results of their reform measures, rather than the nature of their social origins, Middle East rulers are remarkably alike; they share similar historical and political experiences and face many common problems. Iran's so-called White Revolution, for example, emerges, in Bill's analysis, almost exclusively as a gimmick by the Shah to perpetuate himself in power, whereas Nasser's revolution was alleged to be the opposite.[80]

The problem with this kind of approach is that it tends to disregard the perceptions of these rulers themselves and, more importantly, the totality of their experience as this bears upon their actions. In Middle East societies all rulers confront, in varying degrees, the fundamental modern challenges of nation-building, welfare, political participation and authority in the face of the tenacious ideas and practice of traditional Islam. Their response to these challenges cannot be fully appreciated without taking into consideration the continuing need to maintain their freedom of action in the international system to protect the territorial integrity and political independence of the state, in the name of which they act. The new as well as old rulers in the Middle East consist of minorities who monopolize political and economic power, whether they are the Alawis in Syria, the Sunnis in Iraq, or the Farsi-speaking elite in Iran.

The Twin Revolution

In seeking to understand the Middle East, American policymakers should avoid the dangers of "conceptual jails." Some analysts have warned against excessive compartmentalization of domestic and foreign policy in regard to all societies. In the opinion of the participants in the

---

[79] Manfred Halpern, *The Politics of Social Change in the Middle East and North Africa* (Princeton, N.J.: Princeton University Press, 1963), p. 228.

[80] See James A. Bill and Carl Leiden, *The Middle East: Politics and Power* (Boston: Allyn and Bacon, Inc., 1974), pp. 124-155; and James A. Bill, *The Politics of Iran: Groups, Classes and Modernization* (Columbus, Ohio: Charles E. Merrill Publishing Co., 1972), pp. 133-156.

Northwestern Conference on Comparative Politics and International Relations, "the comparative study of the interaction of domestic and foreign politics has quite often been a no-man's land—neglected not because students of politics have thought the topic unimportant but because the divisions between the two fields have tended to foster neglect."[81]

Such neglect would severely harm any effort to understand the foreign policy of Middle East countries. One reason for this is the fact that the very concept of "foreign policy"—like those of "nation," "national interest" and the like—are, in the Western sense of the terms, new to Middle East culture. The Islamic conception of the international system in terms of the "house of war" and the "house of Islam," mentioned before, survived the crusades and subsequently was passed on to the Ottoman Empire, for which no question of foreign policy arose so long as it retained overwhelming military power vis-à-vis Christendom. Despite the Empire's conclusion of treaties with European powers in the sixteenth and seventeenth centuries, not until the eighteenth century did the Ottomans establish resident embassies abroad.[82] The Persians did not do so until the nineteenth century.

In addition to this historical-cultural reason, compartmentalization of foreign and domestic policy can impede better understanding of both because of the nature of developing societies. The personal nature of rulership, the shallowness of modern institutions, the lack of differentiation of roles and functions, the highly foreign-penetrated political system, and similar characteristics all argue against such compartmentalization. Most important of all, detailed empirical analysis can establish the unusually high intensity of interpenetration of foreign and domestic policy decisions in contemporary Middle East societies.[83]

One way of avoiding the problem of compartmentalizing foreign and domestic policies is to start with human action. It is generally recognized in the theory of action that the reality of "choice" is embedded in human action, that of the individual or collectivity.[84] In the Middle East, however, it is most frequently the actions of rulers that are most relevant to the study of their domestic and foreign policies within the context of actual internal and external environments. But as already emphasized, it is the interplay between these environments and the rulers' perceptions of

---

[81] R. Barry Farrell, editor, *Approaches to Comparative and International Politics* (Evanston, Ill: Northwestern University Press, 1966), p. vi.

[82] See Bernard Lewis, *The Middle East and the West* (Bloomington: Indiana University Press, 1964), pp. 115-140.

[83] Examples will be provided below.

[84] See Clyde Kluckhohn, et al., "Values and Value-Orientations in the Theory of Action," in Talcott Parsons and Edward A. Shills, editors, *Toward a Theory of Action* (New York: Harper & Row, 1951), pp. 388-433.

them that is of the greatest importance for a deeper understanding of Middle East behavior—not the action or perception of an abstraction called the "state."

Most leaders of major Middle East societies characterize the totality of their experience today as "revolutionary." "Revolution" may be examined from the standpoints of perception, action and rhetoric. The perceptions of Arab, Iranian and Turkish leaders of "revolution" extend far beyond the notion of radical change "in the system of government,"[85] the most common definition of the term in the West. Whether it is the Arabic term for revolution, *"thawra,"* the Persian *"inqilab,"* or Turkish *"devrimcilik,"* to Middle East leaders revolution concerns fundamental change in both domestic *and* foreign policy. For example, the National Charter of Egypt repeatedly speaks of "many revolutions" confronting Egyptians in their struggle for freedom from exploitation and underdevelopment in "all their material and moral forms."[86]

The perception of the basically twofold nature of revolution, to cite another example, is also evident among the Turks. The well-known "Six Arrows" of the Kemalist revolution may be placed into two basic categories—domestic and foreign policy. The modification of the Kemalist principles in the 1961 Constitution from four to six had no effect on the fact that the Turks still perceive their revolution essentially in terms of foreign and domestic policy. Nasser stated that vision clearly for the Egyptians. He declared:

We are going through two revolutions, not one revolution. Every people on earth goes through two revolutions: a political revolution by which it wrests the right to govern itself from the hand of tyranny, or from the army stationed upon its soil against its will; and a social revolution, involving the conflict of classes, which settles down when justice is secured for the citizens of the united nation.[87]

Nasser often told the Egyptians about their long battle against "foreign and internal despotism," and his successor perceives colonialism and feudalism as "the twin instruments of Egyptian servitude," and considers the word "freedom" in the Egyptian motto to mean Egypt's struggle against foreign control and domestic "exploitation and need."[88]

The Iranian perception of revolution, to cite another example, is also twofold. To be sure, the Shah's "White Revolution" has been nonviolent and "from above," but the point is that it is still part of the perceptions of

---

[85] For this standard definition, see *International Encyclopedia of Social Sciences*, Vol. 13 (1968 edition), p. 501.

[86] For the text of the Charter, see *Middle East News Bulletin*, May 21, 1962.

[87] See Premier Gamal Abdul Nasser, *Egypt's Liberation: The Philosophy of the Revolution* (Washington, D.C.: Public Affairs Press, 1955), pp. 39-40.

[88] Anwar el-Sadat, "Where Egypt Stands," *Foreign Affairs*, October 1972, pp. 114-123.

Middle East leaders; it is regarded by the Shah as "a great social revolution."[89] It aims at radical domestic socio-economic change on the one hand, and an "independent national policy" (i.e., foreign policy) on the other. The fact that fundamental changes in Iran have not been the result of violent or nonviolent destruction of the monarchical regime, as occurred in Iraq and Egypt respectively, does not make it of any less concern or significance. Some Iranians would argue that their revolution has in fact produced greater results than those of Iraq and Egypt. They would also argue that the nonviolent but radical changes that occurred in the United States during the New Deal, and others that occurred in England and Japan, have not disqualified them as "revolutions" just because they were different from what occurred in France in 1789, in Russia in 1917 and in China in 1949.

Regardless of such an argument, the principal point here is that, in the perception of Middle East leaders, domestic and foreign policy are two sides of the same coin. In practice as well, the Middle East experience suggests the interlocking of domestic and foreign policy, as evidenced, for example, by the Iranian nationalist uprisings (the "Constitutional Revolution") of 1905-1911 and the Egyptian struggle under the leadership of Sa'd Zaghlul in 1919.[90]

Middle East rulers have always used a battery of formulas of legitimation. Contemporary leaders use "nationalism," "socialism," "constitutionalism" as well as Islam in validating their domestic and foreign policy decisions and actions. Today, however, in most Middle East societies "revolution" seems to be the favored formula. Just a couple of examples from Egypt and Iran will suffice. Egyptians distinguish *thawra* from *inqilab*: the former conveys the notion of a "real" revolution, while the latter means something more like a coup d'etat, or military coup d'etat (*inqilab askari*). These terms are used for elevating or demeaning supporters or opponents of a regime, as the case may be: *thawra* describes the military takeover of government in Egypt in 1952, and in both Libya and the Sudan in 1969, while *inqilab* is used to refer to the al-Bakr takeover in Iraq in 1968.[91] Domestically, the Sadat regime called the opposition of the Ali Sabri group in 1971 a "conspiracy" (*al-ta'mur*),[92] but labeled its own successful countercoup as "the revolution of May 15," or the "corrective revolution."

---

[89] In writing about the "White Revolution," the Shah has referred to it as a "fundamental and deep-rooted revolution that must completely transform the foundations of the Iranian society." See Rouhollah K. Ramazani, "Iran's 'White Revolution': A Study in Political Development," *International Journal of Middle East Studies*, April 1974, pp. 124-139.

[90] More recent Egyptian and Iranian experiences will be treated later in order to illustrate the intimate interaction between domestic and foreign policy in both of these societies.

[91] See *Al-Ahram*, May 26, and September 1, 1969; and July 18, 1968.

[92] See *al-Mussawar*, May 21, 1971.

The subjective use of the term "revolution" is not confined to Egyptians. Interestingly enough, the Shah calls the launching of his own reform programs a "revolution," and yet this term is not used to characterize the takeover of the government by his own revered father in 1921. The term *inqilab* in Persian is the equivalent of the Arabic *thawra*; there is no term for coup d'etat in Persian as there is in Arabic, and Iranians use the Persianized French term *kudeta* for the Arabic *inqilab*.

The Goals of Domestic and Foreign Policy

Given the close linkage between domestic and foreign policies in the Middle East, it is essential to identify not only foreign policy goals, but the principal domestic ones as well. Gabriel Almond generally identifies four "revolutions" simultaneously facing the leaders of new nations, namely, national, authority, participation and welfare revolutions—and for our purposes these can also be considered as their domestic goals. The primary foreign policy aims of Middle East countries have been identified by a distinguished panel of scholars, under the chairmanship of Raymond Aron, as national survival, which includes national territorial integrity; total independence and freedom from any external control; national prestige; and economic and social progress. To these must be added the aim of Arab unity, insofar as the Arabs are concerned.[93]

Essential to an understanding of these goals is a knowledge of the nature of Middle East societies. Just as, archeologically, Middle East lands reveal a multitude of layers of ancient civilizations, their societies represent the most complicated heterogeneous mosaic of social, tribal, ethnic, economic, religious, linguistic, ideological and political groups. Despite its long history of "national" existence, Iran, for example, is still basically a country of minorities. Since the very concept of "nation" is a recent phenomenon in all Middle East societies, it is difficult, for instance, to speak of Lebanese loyalty to the nation. The devastating civil war in Lebanon today is rooted, in the last analysis, in a basic lack of national accommodation among a multitude of Lebanese factions, sects and groups; there is no consensus on the shape of the modern political system in Lebanon.

Suffice it to state here that in Lebanon, as in all other Middle East societies, the goal of authority emerges most often as the primary concern of the elite. All of these societies, in varying degrees, are chronically on the verge of sociopolitical and territorial disintegration. Islam was born with the message to unite the believers by substituting the bond of faith for

---

[93] See *Sources of Conflict in the Middle East* (London: The Institute for Strategic Studies, Adelphi Papers, No. 26, 1966), p. 11.

their ancient loyalties of blood and other ties, but traditional allegiances to tribe, clan and family, and to sectarian and local communities, coexist to the present day alongside the emerging and spreading consciousness of national loyalties. The processes of modernization have so far tended to contribute more to centrifugal than to centripetal tendencies in most Middle East societies. The explosion of oil prices and the abundance of petrodollars in the oil-producing states and sheikhdoms have spread the processes of socio-economic development to even the remotest tribal societies of the Persian Gulf; they have quickened the unprecedented tempo of change in the more developed ones, and have been accompanied by social, economic and political dislocations. Middle East leaders are bound to encounter the problem of authority on an unprecedented scale.

All Middle East leaders face challenges of basically revolutionary conditions in various forms and degrees. Only in 1975, after nearly a decade and a half, were Kurdish insurgents brought under control in Iraq, and yet the end of the Kurdish problem is not necessarily in sight. Three decades earlier the Kurdish- and Azeri-inhabited provinces of Iran broke off from the rest of the country, with much Soviet and communist support, and formed independent entities.[94] The civil war in Lebanon today threatens partition of the territorial state between Muslim and Maronite-dominated Christian factions.

In most Middle East societies, ethnic, linguistic and religious potential or active fissures are increasingly accompanied by a surging demand for political participation. Neither in the "revolutionary" Egypt of Nasser and Sadat, nor in "conservative" Iran, have the challenges of the alienated middle classes been set to rest, as evidenced by the numerous assassination plots, widespread terrorist violence and assorted coups, perpetrated by all kinds of forces on the left and the right of the political spectrum. Even the presumably most successful participatory regime of the Muslim Middle East, Turkey, has had its large share of dissidence, both violent and nonviolent. And the traditionally highly respected Saudi royal family itself is beginning to feel pressures from the newly emerging middle class—pressures that are bound to grow as a result of the injection of massive amounts of capital, military equipment and technology into Saudi society, particularly since the 1974 agreements with the United States. It is no coincidence that Kuwait, one of the two so-called functioning democracies in the Arab world, began to slide back into authoritarianism in 1976 when the Amir simultaneously dissolved the National Assembly, suspended that part of the constitution requiring early elections, and

---

[94] See Rouhollah K. Ramazani, "The Autonomous Republic of Azerbaijan and the Kurdish People's Republic: Their Rise and Fall," in Thomas T. Hammond, editor, and Robert Farrell, associate editor, *The Anatomy of Communist Takeovers* (New Haven, Conn.: Yale University Press, 1975), pp. 448-474.

issued a decree giving the government greater powers to suspend the newspapers.[95]

Most Middle East leaders do not rule by popular consent as we know the Western political concept. There is no popular consensus on the means and ends of domestic and foreign policy. The lack of a stable political order helps to keep the scale of priorities given to domestic goals in a state of constant flux. Thus, in all these societies, "revolutionary" and "conservative" alike, political modernization lags far behind social and economic development. The former would be likely to shake the very core of the power structure, and no regime proposes to bring about its own demise by political reform detrimental to its hold on power. The notion that without a strong center the whole society may fall apart is no figment of the imagination—no mere rationalization on the part of rulers. Lebanon certainly would not be bleeding to death if it could have maintained a semblance of order while deepening its socio-economic reforms.

The most elementary need today in most developing societies, and particularly in revolutionary Middle East societies, is security. In light of the realities of their existence, Middle East rulers are convinced that security better serves justice than vice versa. In the West, welfare or "human rights," as we define these, may be the real issue of the 1970s—though security was probably the priority issue in the 1940s and 1950s. But we must resist the temptation to project our values, or the so-called universal values on which no real international consensus exists, arbitrarily into the political processes of societies which have different priorities largely because they are living under different conditions. Middle East leaders are, to be sure, muddling through formidable problems that a revolutionary situation has suddenly imposed upon them. One day they may accord the value of social and economic development the highest priority, and the next day they may give priority to the goal of authority. As we shall see from the examples of Egypt and Iran, the reasons for alternating priorities among means and ends can be found by examining the dynamic interaction of various internal and external pressures that constrain decisionmakers rather than scrutinizing the social classes to which various rulers and elites belong.

It should be clear, then, that the problem of instability in Middle East societies does not arise, as it is so often assumed, from the widening gap between the pace of political and economic development alone. Empirically, it can be shown that, just as no Middle East regime has yet offered to commit suicide by undertaking political changes that would be detrimental to its hold on power, none has yet launched programs of socio-

---

[95] *Washington Post*, August 30, 1976.

economic transformation that might well lead to its demise. To do good for their societies, as they see it in the context of their internal and external realities, Middle East leaders tend to cling to governmental control, sometimes at any cost. In all Middle East societies, social and economic modernization programs are targeted principally toward the maintenance of the territorial state and its rulers and elites. This was true in earlier eras, as evidenced in the social and economic reforms under both the Ottoman and Persian states.[96] Even today, as Gabriel Almond puts it, it should be "unambiguously clear that he [a ruler] is not even free to choose the particular mix of revolution or the order which he prefers. Whether he likes it or not, he must give a higher priority to the creation of a nation and of effective government authority before giving way fully to demands for participation and welfare."[97] The danger lies in a perpetual postponement of these other ends, but this danger, no matter how unpalatable to Westerners, is inevitable—the consequence of internal and external revolutionary conditions in Middle East societies usually beyond the control of their leaders.

Does all of this mean that American policymakers should be chiefly concerned with the problem of authority in Middle East societies? Does it mean that the problems of domestic structure and authority determine the foreign policy goals and behavior of Middle East leaders? If we apply Henry Kissinger's general proposition about the relationship of domestic structure to foreign policy in revolutionary societies, the answer would be in the affirmative. Given the nature of these societies, their "uncertain sense of identity," and the near absence of the attributes of nineteenth-century European nations, he contends, "There is a great pressure toward authoritarian rule, and a high incentive to use foreign policy as a means of bringing about domestic cohesion."[98]

But I am not convinced of the validity of his proposition. In the first place, the goal of "domestic cohesion" is synonymous with that of nation-building, which constitutes only one of the four major domestic goals of Middle East leaders—the others being authority, welfare and participation. Second, it is not true that foreign policy, under all circumstances, is simply the instrument of domestic cohesion or any other domestic goal. The preoccupation of Middle East leaders today is with the overriding foreign policy goals of survival and independence of the territorial state. This preoccupation derives today, as in the past, from the strategic

---

[96] See Dankwart A. Rustow, *Politics and Westernization in the Near East* (Princeton, N.J.: Princeton University Press, 1956).

[97] Gabriel A. Almond, *Political Development: Essays in Heuristic Theory* (Boston, Mass.: Little, Brown, 1970), pp. 229-230.

[98] Henry A. Kissinger, "Domestic Structure and Foreign Policy," in James N. Rosenau, editor, *International Politics and Foreign Policy* (New York: The Free Press, 1969), pp. 272-273.

significance of the Middle East region. As George Ball has stated, the Middle East has been

a point of strategic significance from the earliest days when Alexander the Great cast envious eyes on this area. It's the bridge between Europe and Africa. It's an area which dominates the whole southern littoral of the Mediterranean and therefore is the key to the defense of Western Europe. It's an area in which the Soviet Union has had a long interest, ever since the days of the Czar. . . it also happens to contain the greatest pool of energy in the world. So no one can question its vital strategic importance, not only to the United States but practically to every other country.[99]

The Concept of "Autonomy"

Kissinger's theory of foreign policy in revolutionary societies as an instrument of domestic cohesion is not wholly borne out by the facts, at least as far as Middle East societies are concerned. Taking into consideration the long-term and constant pressure of foreign interests on these societies, we can show that the obverse of Kissinger's theory is just as valid, i.e., domestic policy is often used as an instrument of foreign policy. The very processes of domestic Westernization or modernization in the Middle East began in part as a means of defending or maintaining the territorial state. Dankwart Rustow states that "to strengthen the central governments in their contest with European powers was the very purpose of the early measures of Westernization introduced in the Near East in the late eighteenth and early nineteenth century."[100] To be sure, British statesmen, such as Stratford Canning, encouraged Turkish domestic reforms as a means of survival and ensuring the independence of the Ottoman state, but such Turkish leaders as Mustafa Rashid Pasha, Ali and Fuad used domestic reforms primarily as a means of forestalling foreign interference.

The same pattern has persisted to the present time.[101] Egypt's domestic economic "liberalization" and Iran's "White Revolution" were also launched in part for foreign policy ends. The upshot is that, since domestic policy is used for foreign policy aims and foreign policy is used as an instrument of domestic policy, it would be far more realistic for American policymakers to be concerned more about the interplay of the two, and less about one as an instrument of the other under all circumstances.

---

[99] See DOS, News Release, "The Middle East: A Search for Peace," March 6, 1975, p. 1.

[100] Rustow, pp. 17-18.

[101] Cf. Bernard Lewis, *The Emergence of Modern Turkey* (London: Oxford University Press, 1966), and Roderic H. Davison, *Reform in the Ottoman Empire, 1856-1876* (Princeton, N.J.: Princeton University Press, 1963).

A final proposition here is that, since independence is only one of the goals of foreign policy, one must avoid characterizing foreign policy in the Middle East by that goal alone, no matter how important it is. For example, the military build-up of Iran and Saudi Arabia cannot be adequately understood if it is conceived of only with regard to defending the independence of the territorial state against external threats, or, for that matter, internal threats. Another goal of Middle East leaders is prestige, which is obviously related to those of survival and independence, but it is certainly not the same as those other goals. For this important reason it is far more conceptually appropriate and practically useful to focus attention on all goals and actions of Middle East leaders. Toward this end I suggest the concept of "autonomy" as an integrating concept, as a bridge between domestic and foreign policy in the Middle East.

In light of the foregoing discussion, "autonomy" may be defined as the underlying quest of Middle East leaders to increase their freedom of action in behalf of the territorial state *both* within and outside their societies. Within their societies the increase in freedom of action may be aimed at nation-building, welfare, participation and authority. Outside their societies, it may be aimed at survival of the territorial state, political independence and prestige. But the crucial point is that domestic policy may be used for foreign policy ends and foreign policy for domestic ends. Given the intensity of domestic-foreign policy interpenetration on which the concept of autonomy is based, this concept may be quite useful as a guide for thinking more realistically about both foreign and domestic policy in the Middle East. The concept might even have a more general utility in examining the interaction of domestic and foreign policy in other developing societies, but this is not the place to pursue that point. Insofar as Middle East societies are concerned, I would like to offer a few propositions in concluding the theoretical side of this discussion.

First, it is difficult to say which domestic goal or goals are accorded priority over others, because it depends largely on the circumstances as well as on the perceptions and personality of a given policymaker at a given point in time. But in principle, *the goal of authority is accorded a higher priority in Middle East societies*. It often overshadows other domestic aims. Given the nature of their societies, Middle East leaders seem to strive constantly, in response to domestic and/or external pressures, to maintain their control over government and to legitimize it by various means, including coercion and repression. To that extent the goals of welfare and participation, for example, often seem to be used more as means toward the overriding goal of authority than as independent ends.

Second, circumstances as well as the perceptions and personalities of the leaders again play a large role in determining which foreign policy goals are accorded priority over others. But in general *the twin goal of survival-independence is the overriding foreign policy goal*. This is obviously the paramount goal of all states, but in Middle East societies it is a goal far more intensely pursued—mainly for these three reasons: (1) Outside powers for many years have shown great interest in, and exerted heavy pressure on, this strategic area. (2) Survival of regimes is perceived to be inseparable from the survival and independence of the state itself; rulers tend to identify themselves with the state. (3) Most of the Middle East state system is in a revolutionary condition, with Iran and Turkey as two notable exceptions.

The other Middle East countries are in a revolutionary state for two major reasons. The first concerns the unsettled claims of the Arab countries and Palestinians to the state of Israel. For this reason what is still at stake for Israeli leaders is first and foremost the survival of Israel. At stake for most Arab states is their territorial integrity and independence in the face of Israeli occupation of Arab lands since 1967. And at stake for Palestinians is the creation of a Palestinian state. Second, even though Arab unity is often a euphemism for one country's pursuit of its own objectives, the fact remains that the goal of Arab unity is a continuing concern in the Middle East; and the tension between that general goal of Arab unity (*qawmiya*) and the particular goal of independence of individual Arab states (*wataniya*) in effect contributes to the unsettled order of the Middle East system.

Third, *seldom does a ruler or a ruling elite find it necessary to choose between the goals of authority and independence, but if it becomes necessary, the former might be preferred for the short run*. The 1975-1976 Lebanese civil war represents in part such a situation. The Maronite-dominated government of Lebanon, in order to cling to its hold on government, found it necessary to subordinate the political independence of Lebanon to the domestic goal of maintaining its own authority by appearing to make the unusual move of inviting Syrian military intervention to face down the challenge of the so-called leftist Muslim-Palestinian alliance. The Franjieh government seemed to choose, or in fact acquiesced in, the lesser of the two evils. It seemed to subordinate the goal of Lebanese independence to the aim of maintaining its domestic authority with Syrian support, at least for the short run.

5.
Middle East Experience

I T WILL BE useful to see how this empirical empathic approach can assist us in better understanding the nature of foreign policy in the Middle East by applying the concept of "autonomy" to the concrete experience of three very different Middle East societies—Egypt, Iran and Lebanon. Egypt is an Arab country and Iran is non-Arab; one is experiencing revolution from below, the other from above; one is a republic, albeit a one-party system, the other is monarchical; one launched its revolution at the height of the cold war, the other early in the period of detente; one has experienced three wars since the inception of its revolution, the other none; one is economically a poor country, the other is a major oil-producing and resource-rich nation. As contrasted with both Egypt and Iran, Lebanon is a small country; it is religiously less homogeneous and is considered a "confessional democracy"; it is, above all, the most graphic case study of the interplay of domestic and foreign policy in the contemporary Middle East.

Iran

In 1962 the Shah made a major foreign policy decision, namely, to normalize Iran's relations with the Soviet Union. This decision was regarded as "revolutionary" in view of the country's acrimonious relations with the Soviet Union dating back to World War II when Iran was invaded by the Soviet Union in 1941, was pressured for oil concessions in 1944, and was threatened with political disintegration because of Soviet reluctance to withdraw its troops from Iran and Soviet sponsorship of two communist regimes in northern Iran. The Soviet-American global cold war spilled over to intensify the Irano-Soviet cold war once the Shah's regime decided to cast its lot unequivocally with the West through Iran's membership in the Baghdad Pact. The decision of the Shah to normalize relations with the Soviet Union was signaled by Iran's pledge to Moscow not to allow the use of its territory for missile or rocket bases against the Soviet Union.

To be sure, Iran's decision was aimed at reducing its excessive dependence on the United States; acquiring Soviet economic aid in the face of American reluctance to continue budgetary support; neutralizing growing Soviet influence with the hostile revolutionary regime in neighboring Iraq; and increasing Iran's freedom of action or autonomy in world affairs. In addition to these foreign policy goals, however, the decision was also designed to assist the Shah in coping with serious domestic political and economic challenges. The economy was in the grip of rising prices, falling exchange reserves, pervasive waste, inefficiency, and widely-acknowledged corruption. Despite the settlement of the oil nation-alization dispute and subsequent increase in oil revenues, and generous American economic aid during the 1950s, the Shah had failed to per-suade the landed aristocracy to follow his example in land distribution.

It was no coincidence, therefore, that the Shah's new look in world affairs paralleled the launching of an unprecedented land reform pro-gram at home. This program constituted the first "principle" of the Shah's "White Revolution" which now consists of seventeen "principles." The Shah's revolution from above, as with the Free Officers Revolution in Egypt ten years earlier, was based on no particular ideology. The original six principles, like the subsequent ones, were in fact pragmatic programs of social and economic transformation. The Shah's bold decision to undermine the power of the landed aristocracy, which had traditionally constituted one of the main pillars of support of his regime, meant that for the first time since the Constitutional Revolution of 1905-1906 Iran accorded the goal of socio-economic development a higher priority than that of greater freedom of action in world affairs. The circumstances that favored such a choice at the time were the product of a wide variety of factors, ranging from the general improvement in East-West relations and the changing Soviet and American strategic doctrines, to deteriorat-ing domestic economic and political conditions.

But in the wake of the announcement of the historic British decision in 1968 to withdraw forces from the area "East of Suez," including the Persian Gulf, by the end of 1971, foreign policy goals once again were accorded the highest priority. These goals included the protection of not only Iran's external security but also its prestige. This re-emphasis on foreign policy lies at the heart of Iran's massive military build-up in the 1970s, and it is also tied to the regime's aim of maintaining domestic authority while fostering the country's economic growth. To be sure, the explosion of oil prices since 1973 has made it possible for the Shah to afford both ambitious socio-economic development projects and huge military expenditures, but the fact remains that Iran's unprecedented rate of economic growth preceded the sudden rise in oil revenues.[102]

Normalization of relations with the Soviet Union has assisted Iran's programs of domestic socio-economic development in two important ways. First, the USSR has made available to Iran unprecedented commer-cial opportunities. Iran's exports to the Soviet Union now rival its non-oil

---

[102] See Rouhollah K. Ramazani, "Iran's Changing Foreign Policy: A Preliminary Discussion," *The Middle East Journal*, Autumn 1970, pp. 421-437.

exports to both American and European markets. Thanks in part to low transportation costs, the products of Iran's nascent industry can compete successfully in nearby Soviet markets. Second, the Soviets have assisted Iranian socio-economic development through economic and technical cooperation, as evidenced, for example, by Soviet construction of Iran's first steel mill, machine tool plants, hydroelectric dams, and improvement of Caspian Sea ports and fisheries. The more normal, if not cordial, Iranian relations with the USSR have paid off well economically ever since the mid-1960s. After the symbolic no-missile-bases pledge, the Kremlin, which had previously portrayed Iran's every attempt at reform as a hoax of the "rotten monarchical regime," made an about-face and hailed the Shah as a "pioneer in land distribution." Ironically, the Shah's "White Revolution," which, since its inception, has benefited from Soviet economic cooperation, was initially launched in part as an antidote to a Red one.

The foreign policy decision to normalize relations with the Soviet Union was also designed to assist the Shah's regime on the domestic front, politically as well as economically. Amelioration of relations with the Soviet Union would not only increase Iran's maneuverability abroad and assist efforts at rapid socio-economic change at home, but would also facilitate the task of consolidating governmental authority and the Shah's personal power at home. Although the Shah had increasingly tightened his grip over the Iranian political system after the overthrow of the Musaddiq regime in 1953, the sources of opposition to his regime had hardly disappeared, in spite of severe suppression over the next decade. Besides the religiously-based opposition from the Right, the National Frontists and the adherents of the former Communist (Tudeh) Party from the Left were the main sources of anti-Shah opposition in the early 1960s.

The opposition at home seemed all the more menacing in view of open Soviet support. Following the breakdown of Soviet-Iranian negotiations for a long-range nonaggression pact in 1958-1959 and the signing of a new Irano-American defense agreement, Moscow's support of the Shah's domestic opponents increased to the point that Khrushchev himself attacked the Shah personally on two separate occasions. He charged that the Shah feared his own people and was trying to protect his throne with the help of American troops. Politically as well as economically, the Soviet Union dramatically reversed its attitude toward the Shah's regime after he made the no-missile-bases pledge to Moscow. The bloody suppression of the Shah's domestic opponents in June 1963 met with no Soviet criticism; the street riots were conveniently portrayed by Moscow as the product of "reactionary elements."[103]

---

[103] See Ramazani, *Iran's Foreign Policy . . .*, pp. 326-327.

The domestic political structure that was erected in the wake of the June 1963 crisis of authority was scrapped more than a decade later in 1975. The so-called two-party system, represented by the Iran Novin (New Iran) and the Mardom (People's) parties, had proved incapable of striking deep roots in Iranian society. Iran Novin had dominated the political scene as an arm of the government. The government blamed the failure of the two-party system on the ineptness of the opposition while, in effect, admitting that there was no real opposition party. Only four days before his sudden agreement with Saddam Husain in Algiers settling the long-standing Irano-Iraqi conflict, the Shah surprised the Iranian people as well as government officials by his unexpected decision to dissolve both parties and create in their place the new "Iran Resurgence Party" (Hizb-e Rastakhiz-e Iran).

The new party was declared to be based on three cardinal principles: the Constitution, the Monarchy, and the White Revolution.[104] All Iranians were urged to join the party. They had three "alternatives": to join the party, to oppose the party actively, and to stay out of the party without actively opposing it. Those Iranians who would opt for the second alternative were advised to leave the country or be put in jail, and those who would choose the third could be tolerated, though not favored, by the regime. The uncertainty of the situation was reflected in the variety of responses by the people and the government. What is of interest here is the unresolved crisis of authority that is still present in "conservative" Iran as it is in "revolutionary" Egypt. There is, for example, a striking resemblance between the Shah's attempt to consolidate his authority by establishing a single party organization and President Sadat's tinkering with the structure of the Arab Socialist Union (ASU) basically toward the same end.

While the Shah's decision to normalize relations with the Soviet Union has over the past decade contributed to some basic domestic socio-economic changes and greater consolidation of his own authority, these have in turn strengthened Iran's capability to operate with greater freedom of action in the international system. It is no coincidence that during the past decade Iran has become the preponderant power in the Persian Gulf area.[105] Iran's considerable influence in the international system is in part a byproduct of the conjunction of favorable domestic and international circumstances. The Shah has skillfully utilized the opportunity afforded

---

[104] The Shah's sudden announcement about the "restructured political system" was made to newspaper editors, publishers, and the leaders of the political parties at Niravan Palace. For the text of his address, see *Ittila'at*, March 3, 1975. For a complete report of it in English, see *Kayhan*, March 3, 1975.

[105] For Iran's resurgence in regional affairs, see Rouhollah K. Ramazani, "Emerging Patterns of Regional Relations in Iranian Foreign Policy," *Orbis*, Winter 1975, pp. 1043-1069; and Ramazani, *The Persian Gulf: Iran's Role* (Charlottesville: University Press of Virginia, 1972).

by this convergence to pursue the goals of what he calls Iran's "independent national policy." He claims that this policy is a byproduct of his White Revolution, but these foreign and domestic policies have their roots in complicated, yet on the whole favorable, internal and external circumstances. Iran's situation, however, remains one of uncertainty regarding the future of its domestic stability and international resurgence and its response over the long run to the fundamental economic, political, intellectual and psychological challenges of the modern age.

Egypt

Few developments in Egypt's foreign policy in recent years can match President Sadat's momentous decision to launch the October War and then boldly conclude two separate agreements with Israel in the war's aftermath. Most of the existing literature on the war concentrates on the external factors underlying Sadat's decision to go to war, yet even a lengthy exposition of these factors leaves much to be desired. Any serious analysis of these factors must include the limitations placed on the American pre-war peace initiative, because U.S. statesmen were constrained by domestic politics from going beyond efforts to induce Israel to accept the so-called Rogers Plan, and because America was preoccupied with the war in Southeast Asia. Other external factors would have to include the impact of detente and of Soviet willingness eventually to meet Egyptian demands for Soviet arms and involvement, following the slowdown of Soviet arms supply in the wake of the expulsion of Soviet advisers in 1972. No less important were the pressures from Libya, which provided Egypt with a $150 million annual subsidy; the Israeli reluctance to go beyond grudging acceptance of the U.S. peace initiative; and the Egyptian alarm concerning the annexationist program of the Israeli Labor Party. No matter how one views the impact of these and other external factors, such as the energy crisis, on Sadat's war decision, the point here is that his overriding and immediate foreign policy objective of recovering the territories lost in the Six-Day War was closely linked to the unresolved domestic economic, political and other problems of the Egyptian Revolution.

Domestic socio-economic development, for example, had received considerable priority before the Six-Day War in 1967 with some degree of success.[106] Before the war most foreign aid (averaging about 2.5 per cent

---

[106] For the best economic account of the Egyptian Revolution during its first decade, see Charles Issawi, *Egypt in Revolution: An Economic Analysis* (London: Oxford University Press, 1963). For the economic consequences of the Six-Day War, see E. Kanovsky, "The Economic Aftermath of the Six-Day War," *The Middle East Journal*, Spring 1968, pp. 131-143, and E. Kanovsky, "The Economic Aftermath of the Six-Day War: UAR, Jordan and Syria," *ibid.*, Summer 1968, pp. 278-296.

of the GNP) had been used for economic development rather than military purposes.[107] From July 1960 up to the Six-Day War, Egypt experienced a period of accelerated development, as evidenced by the average annual increase in the gross national product of 6 per cent in real terms; by the rise in the standard of living by 3-4 per cent a year; and by the rise of industrial output as a proportion of the GNP from 17 per cent to 20-22 per cent in the mid-sixties. The Six-Day War radically transformed Egyptian priorities with the result that the pre-war defense expenditure of an average of 8-10 per cent of the GNP increased to at least 25 per cent in the 1967-1975 period, and simultaneously the gross national product rose only by about 3 per cent a year in real terms; gross investment declined to 13 per cent of the GNP and the standard of living rose only by about 2 per cent a year. In other words, the foreign policy goal of recovering the lost territories overshadowed the domestic goals of fundamental and rapid socio-economic development, although the latter were not abandoned.

On the domestic front, the unresolved problem of authority was no less significant than the problem of socio-economic development prior to the October War. The 1952 coup d'etat had overthrown the incumbent king, but the establishment of a new order was seriously challenged even before the Six-Day War, as evidenced by Nasser's preoccupation with suppressing anti-revolutionary elements—including the *Ikhwan*, communists, Naguib and his supporters, Wafdists and other so-called vestiges of pre-revolutionary rule.[108] Yet it was the shock of the Six-Day War that revealed the unresolved sociopolitical problems of the Revolution. The legitimacy of the revolutionary regime was seriously challenged by vociferous demands for change (*taghyir*) and by manifestations of unrest— ranging from assassination plots, planned coups, and chronic cabinet reshuffling to ideological attacks on Nasser by the Marxist-Leninists, Maoists, and the Muslim Brotherhood. The brutal collapse of Nasser's image as a "son of Egypt" after the disastrous defeat in the 1967 war was reflected in the new crude reference to him as *al-wahsh* ("the wild beast").[109] The war did not cause the crisis of authority in revolutionary Egypt, but added to it the new crisis of autonomy as the result of the presence of alien forces on Egyptian soil. The Egyptian leader recovered a small measure of respect and even affection after the cease-fire that

---

[107] This fact and the following information in this paragraph are drawn from Middle East Information Media, *Middle-East Intelligence Survey*, July 15, 1975, pp. 57-59.

[108] For contrasting assessments of Nasser's charismatic leadership, see R. Hrair Dekmejian, *Egypt Under Nasir: A Study in Political Dynamics* (Albany: State University of New York Press, 1971); and John P. Entelis, "Nasser's Egypt: The Failure of Charismatic Leadership," *Orbis*, Summer 1974, pp. 451-464.

[109] This account is based on Shimon Shamir, *Nasser and Sadat, 1967-1973: Two Approaches to the Crisis*, Occasional Papers, The Shiloah Center for Middle Eastern and African Studies, Tel Aviv University, December 26-31, 1974.

ended the so-called War of Attrition in 1970, but in many ways Nasser's effectiveness was a victim of the 1967 disaster.

His successor, President Sadat, was no less conscious of the close relationship between the problem of authority at home and the recovery of lost territories from Israel. His peace offensive, like that of his predecessor, aimed simultaneously at regaining the lost territories, consolidating his own control, and buying Egypt a breathing spell for concentrating efforts on staggering problems of socio-economic development. The failure of his peace initiatives meant that the sacred foreign policy goal of territorial integrity would remain unfulfilled and that the multitude of domestic problems would continue to undermine the nation's stability.

The problem of authority in particular haunted Sadat before the October War. His spectacular victory against his opponents within the Arab Socialist Union (ASU), particularly against the Ali Sabri faction in May 1971, helped to consolidate his power as the new leader of Egypt since his popular election in 1970 to the presidency, but the crisis of authority nevertheless intensified in the context of the no-peace, no-war situation. He outflanked his leftist opponents by signing the treaty with the Soviet Union in 1971,[110] and placated his critics from the Right by expelling Soviet advisers in 1972, but neither move resolved the basic domestic sociopolitical problems. For example, the army's dissatisfaction with the presence of Soviet advisers led to the reported uprising at the army base near Suez, resulting in the dismissal of General Ahmad Sadiq and some ten other high-ranking officers. The restlessness of the army officers, caused largely by the state of continuous mobilization, was matched by the frustration of students and their journalist sympathizers as the result of the President's unfulfilled promises to terminate the no-war, no-peace state of affairs. The "Year of Decision"—1971—had ended in agonizing indecision.

The same patterns of interplay between foreign and domestic policy that were noticeable in waging war have been present during the course of Sadat's momentous decisions to conclude two agreements with Israel since the October War. To be sure, the remarkable secrecy of planning for the October War, both diplomatically and militarily, the relatively creditable performance of the Egyptian military during this war as compared with the Six-Day War, and the destruction of Israel's Bar-Lev line after the spectacular crossing of the canal, did a great deal to assuage the injured sense of pride of not only the Egyptians but all Arabs.

However, enormous problems of socio-economic change and political modernization continue to haunt Sadat in the course of his search for

---

[110] See Nadav Safran, "The Soviet-Egyptian Treaty—As Seen from Washington," *New Middle East*, July 1971, pp. 10-13.

peace. The interplay of these problems with that of recovering the lost territories is reflected in parallel developments in Egypt's diplomatic reorientation and simultaneous attempts at political and economic liberalization. In 1975 Egypt owed the outside world about $11 billion and its balance-of-payments deficit stood at $3 billion. The agreements with Israel as well as the overall diplomatic reorientation are perceived as steps toward eventually recovering the lost territories and toward attracting American, West European, Iranian and Arab aid for fulfilling domestic goals. It is also hoped that these measures will help to attract investment, particularly by American businessmen—a prospect which had been present since the 1960s, but conditions for which had never been realized. The reopening of the Suez Canal and the planned reconstruction of the canalside cities all reflect an increasing effort to accord the goal of domestic socio-economic development at least the high priority that it seemed to enjoy prior to the Six-Day War. Economic liberalization, or "the policy of economic openness" as the Egyptians call it, might have a fair chance of reversing the trends that prevailed from 1967 to 1973, depending on Egypt's ability to attract up to $3 billion of Western and Arab (oil) money. But all this remains to materialize and meanwhile pressing problems of political institutionalization show little sign of abatement.

The popular support gained by President Sadat, largely as the result of the October War, is as vulnerable to the vicissitudes of adverse internal and international circumstances as the seemingly unassailable charisma of his predecessor. The core problems of political institutionalization are no less acute in Egypt than in Iran. The array of political structures, ranging from the Liberation Rally of 1953-1956 to the National Union of 1956-1961, and finally to the Arab Socialist Union since 1961, has on the whole proved a failure in meeting demands for genuine political participation. Nasser always believed that order had to precede a multiparty system, but this fluid situation has continued down to the present. The Sadat regime continues, after the October War as before it, to balance domestic forces, to reshuffle cabinets, and to play one faction off against another in the incessant struggle for power and consolidation of authority. The opposition to the government consists generally of communists, appearing under all sorts of labels ranging from "the Patriots" to "the Democrats"; the so-called neo-Nasserites who are suspected of getting aid and comfort from the Libyan leader; and the militant Islamic groups, including remnants of the banned Muslim Brotherhood.

The domestic political policies of the Sadat regime, like its economic policies, are complicated enormously by the ebb and flow of the volatile regional and international environment. For example, after the breakdown of the American peace mission in March 1975 and the consequent increase of dissatisfaction among the military in Egypt with the slow pace of Sadat's diplomacy, he appointed General Muhammad Husni Mubarak to the position of Vice-President in April, leading to considerable speculation about the participation of the military in decision-making. But after the conclusion of the second Egyptian-Israeli disengagement agreement, such speculation diminished. Instead, it appeared that the twenty-year-old monopoly of political organization held by the regime was beginning to break down. In August 1975 Sadat emphasized that there was no place for political parties in Egypt; the only legitimate political action was that which accepted the principle of national unity and adhered to the tenets of the 1952 Revolution. It is worth noting the remarkable resemblance between Sadat's attitude and that of the Shah regarding his new Rastakhiz Party.

More recently (1976), "political platforms" have proliferated within the ASU. Whether or not these "platforms" may be regarded as possible nuclei of future political parties in Egypt remains to be seen. All that is certain at the moment is that their legalization by the regime may be a sign of embryonic political pluralism. More important, the campaign for seats in Egypt's national legislative body, the People's Assembly, in October 1976 was regarded as perhaps "the freest in the country's history," despite Sadat's control of the ASU. He himself has said that Egypt is not ready for unrestricted democracy in the American style, but the political atmosphere is "far more liberal" than it was under President Nasser. I doubt, however, that Sadat's gradual political liberalization will work. Street riots and terrorism by religious fanatics in 1977 may well force him to reconsider that goal before long.

Lebanon

Few examples in contemporary Middle East history illustrate as tragically as the Lebanese example does the failure of a ruling elite to cope simultaneously with problems of foreign and domestic policy. These problems lie at the heart of the 1975-1976 civil war. The crisis was sparked on April 13, 1975, by an exchange of gunfire between Palestinians and Phalangists outside a church in the Ain-Rummaneh quarter of Beirut, which spread to the Burj al Barjna refugee camps and to Tripoli, resulting in 100 deaths in a couple of days. Since then, many thousands have died and many have left their homes, and the world is watching with great anxiety the cease-fire established in October 1976 in the wake of the Riyadh and Cairo meetings. At the start of the civil war the predominantly Christian Phalange Party, the biggest and best-organized in Lebanon, had over 80,000 members, including a 5,000-strong, heavily-armed militia. Total Palestinian fighting strength was estimated at between 20,000 and 25,000, although there were some 450,000 Palestinians in Lebanon, including about 100,000 in the 15 refugee camps that were set up in 1948 after the creation of Israel.

The latest Palestinian-Phalange fighting, however, was preceded by another outbreak of an indigenous, age-old conflict in Lebanese society. The incident that set off this conflict was the "Proteine Affair" of February 1975, when strikes and demonstrations were launched by predominantly Muslim fishermen in Sidon in opposition to an attempted usurpation of their rights by a private company formed under the chairmanship of the former Maronite Christian President of Lebanon, Camille Chamoun. The incident acted as a catalyst, bringing into the open the grievances of Muslim leaders against the wielders of power in the existing political system. They reiterated their long-standing appeal for structural changes in the National Charter in order to curb the powers of the president in government and the Maronite Christians in the Lebanese army.

Domestic political as well as foreign policy problems, however, had their roots in the very birth of the state of Lebanon, especially in the 1943 National Charter. On the basis of a French-conducted census in 1932, the various Christian sects combined were considered to have a slight majority over the Muslims and, hence, the 1943 Charter fixed the parliamentary representation at a constant ratio of six Christians to five Muslims; the President of the Republic, the most powerful political figure, was to be a Maronite Christian; the Prime Minister was to be a Sunni Muslim; and the Speaker of the Chamber of Deputies, a Shi'i Muslim. Although this political system was a delicately balanced combination of several sectarian interests, the Maronite Christians were assured a predominant political role. The same sectarian ratio was also applied to every appointment for public office. More important, the army's commander-in-chief and many senior officer cadres were solidly Maronite.

Lebanon was thus born as a Christian state. As such, it was to be independent and to follow a foreign policy which would not be inconsistent with the interests of its Arab neighbors; the Christians were not to look to outside support, and particularly were not to call on France as their protector; and the Muslims were to give up their demands to become part of Syria.[111] No real, widespread consensus on these fundamental principles has been achieved in Lebanon since the creation of the state.

---

[111] See Ralph E. Crow, "Religious Sectarianism in the Lebanese Political System," *Journal of Politics*, August 1962, p. 517. For other useful works on the background of the Lebanese civil war, see Michael C. Hudson, "A Case of Political Underdevelopment," *ibid.*, November 1967, pp. 821-837; Samir Khalaf, "Primordial Ties and Politics in Lebanon," *Middle East Studies*, January 1967, pp. 243-269; David R. Smock and Audrey C. Smock, *The Politics of Pluralism: A Comparative Study of Lebanon and Ghana* (New York: Elsevier, 1975); Norman Howard, "Upheaval in Lebanon," *Current History*, January 1976, pp. 5-9 and 36; and Enver M. Khoury, *The Crisis in the Lebanese System: Confessionalism and Chaos* (Washington, D.C.: American Enterprise Institute for Public Policy Research, 1976).

On the contrary, all internal and external developments have contributed more to communal and subcommunal conflict than to the emergence of anything like *e pluribus unum*, one national community out of many.

One of the most persistent political characteristics of Lebanon before and since the most recent civil war has been the determination of the Maronite ruling elite to perpetuate itself in power and to preserve the individuality of the Lebanese state under its control. The civil war of 1958 marked the first major challenge to Maronite control of domestic and foreign policy. Regional political divisions between the pan-Arab Nasserites and the Lebanese particularists, between the "revolutionary" and "reactionary" Arab regimes, and between the "pro-Western" and "anti-Western" states and groups within the Middle East, combined with the traditional communal and subcommunal divisions within Lebanon, triggered the civil war. President Chamoun's endorsement of the Eisenhower Doctrine was regarded by his opponents within and outside Lebanon as a violation of the tenets of Lebanese foreign policy, that is, Lebanon's "neutrality" in the cold war. His appeal for American intervention was to insure both the predominance of the Maronite Christians in domestic politics and their maintenance of a "pro-Western" foreign policy orientation in international politics.

The first civil war brought into the open a frank discussion about the Charter. By 1958 the 1932 population census was severely challenged, because the Muslims believed that they comprised an absolute majority and the Shi'i Muslims, rather than the Maronites, constituted the largest minority in Lebanese society. But the traditional sectarian conflict and the demographic change were not the only factors contributing to the crisis. Although the civil war was discussed in sectarian terms—Muslim against Christian—it could not conceal "the underlying movement of discontent and demands for a more balanced and equitable dispensation of the national wealth."[112] The failure of the ruling elite to meet the rising demands for socio-economic change aggravated the basic sectarian, personal, familial and other conflicts.

The confessional, communal, socio-economic, sociopolitical and cultural divisions of Lebanese society were aggravated even further by the emergence of the Palestinian operations against Lebanon after the 1967 and 1973 Arab-Israeli wars. The disastrous 1967 war and Arab humiliation left a power vacuum that the Palestinian commandos tried to fill. I witnessed the enthusiasm with which the Lebanese Muslims in 1968 received the news of the successful Palestinian stand, with Jordanian support, against the Israeli forces at the battle of Karamah. This Palestinian show of force at a time of low morale throughout the Arab world

---

[112] David Waines, "The Anatomy of a Crisis," *International Perspectives*, January/February 1976, pp. 14-20.

increased the Palestinian appeal to various groups in Lebanon. The original gains that the Palestinians achieved in Lebanon, however, were due in part to the help of Syria; and after the rise of Hafez Assad to power in 1970, his regime placed restrictions on guerrilla operations from Syria, whether they were aimed at Jordan or Israel.

Before the 1973 Arab-Israeli war, two other developments made the Palestinian presence in Lebanon a greater threat than ever to the Maronite state. First, the Palestinian raids into Israel from Lebanon, or the "Fatahland," named after the main faction within the Palestine Liberation Organization (PLO), increasingly invited Israeli reprisals into Lebanese territory. The relative immunity from the consequences of armed conflict with Israel that the Maronites had achieved by staying out of three Arab-Israeli wars was now severely eroded. The Maronite ruling elite would have preferred to have nothing to do with the Palestinians, but it did not have much choice. Under Arab, particularly Egyptian, pressures, the Lebanese government agreed to the "Secret Cairo Accord" of 1969. Although the accord presumably regulated the commando operations against Israel and Israeli-held Syrian territory, it did recognize their "right" to operate from designated areas in Lebanon. Second, King Hussein of Jordan demolished the Palestinian presence in his kingdom in 1970-1971 by means of a bloody crackdown on the commandos, which they still remember as "Black September." Just as this development increased the strategic value of Lebanon to the commandos, it aggravated the problem of the Palestinian presence for the Lebanese government.

The emergence of the PLO as an actor in world affairs between the Arab-Israeli war of 1973 and the spring of 1975 continued to intensify domestic and foreign policy problems for the Lebanese ruling elite. Although the Palestinians lacked a permanent territorial base, a unified leadership and a well-integrated community, the "Palestinian revolution" (*thawrat filistin*) gained considerable prestige at the 1974 Arab summit meeting in Rabat, and their recognition at the United Nations further increased their appeal to like-minded Muslim and leftwing groups within Lebanon. In the early stages of the Lebanese conflict between the government and the groups attached to the leftist and Muslim alliance, the PLO appeared to try to avoid being sucked into the conflict, as evidenced by its memorandum to the National Dialogue Committee which stated that its aim was still to return to Palestine and its desire was to preserve "Lebanese security, stability and independence as well as its sovereignty, national unity and integrity."[113] But their attitude changed by January 1976 when forces of the right-wing Phalange Party and National Liberal Party (NLP) blockaded the Palestinian Tal Zaatar and Jisr al-Pasha refugee camps.

---

[113] *Arab Report & Record*, October 1-15, 1975.

These blockades strengthened the PLO's alliance with the Muslim and leftist elements under the leadership of Kamal Jumblatt. Under their alliance, the armed forces of Arafat and Jumblatt were lined up against the Franjieh government on the one hand, and the Christian extremists and President Hafez Assad of Syria on the other.

Syria threw its lot in with the Lebanese government for a variety of reasons. These include Syria's historic interest in a Greater Syrian scheme consisting of Palestine, Syria, Lebanon and Jordan; its hatred of the Iraqi Ba'athist regime that supported the "rejectionist" front of the Palestinians; Hafez Assad's feud with President Sadat because of the latter's alleged betrayal of the Arab cause by concluding the second Sinai disengagement agreement with Israel in September 1975; Syrian concern with being sucked into another war with Israel, not of its own choosing and timing, if the extreme left and the Palestinians succeeded in dominating the Lebanese government; and Assad's own fear that, if such a government should emerge in Lebanon at the expense of the Maronite minority, his own Alawi minority control in Syria might be subjected to pressures from the Sunni majority and the extremist wing of the Syrian Ba'ath party, sympathetic to the Iraqi Ba'ath party.[114]

In the civil war of 1958 the Chamoun government had sought to extricate itself from domestic and foreign policy problems by inviting American military intervention. In the 1975-1976 civil war the Franjieh government relied reluctantly on Syrian military intervention to end the civil war, to uphold Maronite control of government, and to insure the survival of the Christian state. The fact that the Franjieh government had little choice in the matter did not detract from the Maronite determination to achieve these goals. In his inaugural speech of September 1976, President Elias Sarkis sought to legitimize the Syrian military presence by stressing that the Syrian forces had been "invited" to enter Lebanon.[115] But it was also an attempt on his part to legitimize the Maronite authority and to reassert ultimately the independence of Lebanon. It is also important to note, however, that only after the outbreak of the civil war and just before the large-scale Syrian military intervention did the Franjieh government attempt to introduce, belatedly and half-heartedly, some domestic sociopolitical reforms.

The same extremism that marked the conflict between Muslim and Christian forces on the battlefield was reflected in demands for reform. For example, the self-styled "progressive" Lebanese parties, including representatives of the Progressive Socialist Party, the Lebanese Communist Party, the Arab Communist Organization, and the Ba'ath Party,

---

[114] See James M. Markham, "Lebanon: The Insane War," *New York Times* Magazine, August 15, 1976.
[115] *New York Times*, September 24, 1976.

called on August 18, 1975, for the end of the confessional system, the reform of the administration and the electoral system, the reorganization of the army, and the election of a constituent assembly. A few days later the Phalangist leader, Pierre Gemayel, told President Franjieh that the National Charter should not be amended or abolished without the unanimous agreement of the Lebanese people; secularization of the state should be achieved before confessionalism was abolished; and the army was the most important national institution and should be reinforced.[116]

Repeated attempts at dialogue between the government and the extremist factions of "the left" and "the right" bore little fruit. A 17-point reform program, labeled the "Constitutional Document," was adopted by the Lebanese Council of Ministers in February 1976. Meeting of Muslim demands for reform of the political system was apparently balanced against meeting of Christian demands for control over the activities of the Palestinian guerrillas. The reforms appeared at first to have been favorably received, as they gave the Muslims several major concessions. The Sunni Premier would now be elected by a simple majority in the Chamber of Deputies in which the Muslims and Christians would be equally represented. In the past, the Premier had been appointed by the Maronite Christian President. The reforms also would ensure greater power-sharing between Muslims and Christians in the sense that an indirect attempt would be made to abolish confessionalism in the administrative system traditionally dominated by the Maronite Christians.[117]

The extremists on the left and the right of the political spectrum, however, rejected various points of the new program. The extreme right-wing "Guardians of the Cedars," for example, rejected the notion that Lebanon was Arab; they contended that it was Phoenician, and considered the 1969 Cairo agreement governing the presence of Palestinians in Lebanon as null and void, warning that "the struggle will not end until all the Palestinians have left Lebanon."[118] The Druze Socialist leader, Kamal Jumblatt, also decried the proposed reforms as inadequate, since they were addressed only to superficial symptoms rather than to the root causes of the crisis.

Between the rejection of the Syrian-sponsored proposals for political reforms and the election of Elias Sarkis as President of Lebanon on May 8, 1976, two major developments occurred that helped to shape the civil war. One was the disintegration of the Lebanese army that began on March 11 with the strangest and most complex coup d'etat in the history of the Middle East. The Beirut Military Governor, Muslim Brigadier 'Aziz

---

[116] See *Arab Report & Record*, August 16-31, 1975.
[117] *Ibid.*, February 1-14, 1976.
[118] *Ibid.*, February 15-29, 1976.

al-Ahdab, stressed his intention to dissolve the government and sack President Franjieh, who had technically been removed by the parliamentary election of Sarkis as President, but who refused to resign until the end of his term of office in September 1976. The other development, mentioned earlier, was the tacit line-up of Palestinian forces—with the exception of As-Saiqa—including the "rejectionist" forces of George Habash and the Fatah forces of Arafat with those of the leftist Muslim forces under Jumblatt, against the Lebanese government and the separate forces of the Christian alliance and Syria. These developments, coupled with Syrian military intervention first by proxy and then openly, changed the shape and scope of the civil war. The earlier conflicts between Muslims and Christians, between "leftists" and "rightists," and between leftists and the Lebanese government, now took the form of an armed conflict primarily between the Muslim forces of the leftist-Palestinian alliance on the one hand and the Christian forces on the other.

Any generalization about the complex, chaotic and perplexing Lebanese situation today is bound to be an over-simplification, but these basic patterns of the conflict have generally persisted to the present time. There are indications that the 57th cease-fire, imposed as the result of the six-sided summit meeting held in Riyadh involving Saudi Arabia, Syria, Egypt, the PLO, Kuwait and Lebanon, might hold, but whether a united, sovereign and independent Lebanon can re-emerge from the ashes of the catastrophic civil war is problematical.

In the vastly different context of the international system of the 1970s, as contrasted with the late 1950s, the United States did not intervene militarily in the 1975-1976 Lebanese civil war as it did in the 1958 civil war. American policy toward the recent civil war was guided by the basic tenets of the Guam Doctrine—the United States will not try to police the world. However, the United States has been deeply involved in efforts aimed primarily at ending the civil war and containing it so it does not lead to another Arab-Israeli conflict. Toward these primary aims, the United States in principle discouraged any "unilateral intervention" by Israel or Syria, but as time went by it appeared that Syrian intervention was a lesser evil than either a dismembered Lebanon or one dominated by the radical forces of the leftist-Palestinian alliance. The United States has in effect relied upon Syrian and Israeli restraint for the settlement of the Lebanese civil war. In addition to its own direct mediatory efforts, chiefly the mission of Ambassador Dean Brown[119] and the fact-finding mission of Robert Houghton and David Mack, two American diplomats, the United

---

[119] See the address by L. Dean Brown, "Lebanon—A Mission of Conciliation," Middle East Institute, Washington, D.C., June 22, 1976. I would like to acknowledge my indebtedness to Ambassador Brown, who gave me an interview on the topics covered in his address.

States supported what I may call President Sadat's "letter diplomacy"[120] and "hands-off" policy as well as the mediatory efforts of Kuwait, Saudi Arabia and the Arab League.

The success or failure of the most recent cease-fire, imposed after the Riyadh summit and the Cairo meeting of the Arab League, will make a great difference in the resumption of American peacemaking efforts in the Arab-Israeli conflict. As Secretary Kissinger put it, the process of peacemaking has been interrupted since the end of March 1976. "I believe," the Secretary stated, "that as the situation in Lebanon settles down, it will be possible to begin this process of exploration again. . . . I believe that progress toward peace in the Middle East is possible. . . ."[121]

---

[120] My review of the Egyptian newspaper, *al-Ahram*, from the beginning of the Lebanese crisis reveals that President Sadat dispatched numerous letters to various Lebanese leaders.

[121] *Department of State Bulletin*, June 14, 1976, p. 749.

6.
Conclusions

THE CENTRAL QUESTION before us is whether President Carter's conception of a Middle East peace will be adequate. We noted earlier that the President's views have been influenced significantly by the Brookings Institution study, which is premised on the inadequacy of Kissinger's step-by-step approach. The criticism of that approach has been for the most part based on the "tactical, piecemeal and *ad hoc*" nature of Kissinger's diplomacy and its failure to address itself to "the essential issues" of the Arab-Israeli conflict. The President's "comprehensive" approach will presumably address itself to all the parties and all the essential issues of the conflict, and hence it may enable the present Administration to plot a more consistent as well as comprehensive strategy.

In addition to the requirements of the Arab recognition of Israel and the Israeli withdrawal of forces from Arab lands, the President's conception so far has included two other prerequisites of peace in the Middle East: (1) the need for a Palestinian "homeland," and (2) open borders, trade, travel and cultural exchange between the Arab states and their Israeli neighbor. Although it is too early to state at the time of this writing, when the President has not yet completed his preliminary talks with all Arab leaders, how his emerging conception of a Middle East peace will be received, President Sadat's reaction so far has been generally encouraging to the Administration. During his visit to Washington in April 1977, he dropped his previous view that there could be a normalization of relations with Israel only in the next generation, and instead he envisaged that "full normalization" of relations with Israel was possible within about five years after a Geneva agreement had been signed, and some interim steps toward normal relations could be taken even earlier.

President Carter's emerging conception of a Middle East peace will probably be more "comprehensive" than that of former Secretary Kissinger's because it seems to address all the essential issues of the conflict *at the very outset*. Yet the extent to which Carter's approach is likely to be more successful than his predecessor's is difficult to predict, for his search for peace is still in its embryonic phase. Nevertheless, on the basis of what we know now about the President's conceptual framework, it is abundantly clear that his ideas, as Kissinger's before him, are not conducive to developing a comprehensive, coherent and realistic conception of U.S. policy in the entire Middle East.

My objective in this study has been to demonstrate that (1) the essential issues of the Arab-Israeli conflict today, no matter how crucial in themselves, cannot be neatly separated from the urgent problems in the

Middle East region as a whole, and (2) there is a great need for a complete rethinking of U.S. policy and the development of a comprehensive conceptual framework for Middle East policy so that American policymakers are no longer dealing with artificially compartmentalized issues. The urgency of this need derives basically from the breakdown of the traditional distinction between the "confrontation" and other Arab states because of two major linkages that have developed between the problems of American policy in the Persian Gulf area and Arab-Israeli zone. These have resulted from the nature of the U.S. response to the Arab oil embargo on the one hand, and the massive American arms sales in the Gulf area on the other. A future Middle East war would probably spread swiftly to the Gulf area, and, if it did, it would have catastrophic consequences for the entire Middle East, for the flow of oil supplies to world markets, and hence for international peace and security. A future peace in the Middle East would remain largely illusory unless conceived at the outset with a view not only to settling the essential issues of the Arab-Israeli conflict, but also to providing the foundation for stability and security in the Middle East as a whole.

The basic prerequisite of a comprehensive and realistic conception of U.S. policy in the region is *a genuine recognition of Middle East states as potential builders of a stable regional order*. From the announcement of the Truman Doctrine and the Greek-Turkish aid program to the Guam Doctrine, the American conception of the Middle East was dominated by the concern with Soviet expansionist aspirations and policies in the region. The area was perceived primarily as a major strategic arena of the global competition with the Soviet Union. The importance of the Middle East states to the United States consisted in the contribution they could make to American efforts to contain Soviet power and influence in the Middle East.

The U.S. commitment to the survival of Israel was regarded for the most part as a strategic imperative, despite undeniable humanitarian and political considerations as well; the overthrow of the nationalist government of Dr. Musaddiq in favor of the Shah's regime was hailed as an American strategic gain in the cold war, despite the popular anti-Americanism that it entailed; Iraq was included in the American-sponsored Baghdad Pact, despite the anticipated intensification of ancient divisions within the Arab world; the Anglo-French-Israeli invasion of Egypt was opposed mainly for fear of the extension of Soviet power and influence to the Eastern Mediterranean, despite the predictable rift that would develop between the United States and its NATO allies; the Chamoun government was propped up by means of American intervention aimed primarily at the containment of "international communism" under the Eisenhower Doctrine, despite its deepening effects upon ancient communal divisions within Lebanese society; and the spectacular victory of Israel against Egypt in the 1967 war was welcomed in Washington as a means of checkmating simultaneously the further expansion of Soviet power and of Nasserism in the Middle East. Under all these circumstances, the states of the region were perceived primarily as the objects of great-power politics in the strategic Middle East.

Did the end of a long and complicated process of British imperial demise in the Middle East in 1971 change this basic American conception of the states of the area? The United States decided, in the wake of the 1968 British decision to withdraw forces from the area "East of Suez," *not* to try to replace British power in the Persian Gulf area. Instead, Washington preferred to accord Iran and Saudi Arabia the primary responsibility for maintaining security in this area. This "twin-pillar" policy provided the basis for American assistance to these two "key" Persian Gulf states to build up their military capabilities. This policy seemed compatible with the tenets of the Guam Doctrine which called for the devolution of American global responsibilities to regional powers. However, the choice of Iran and Saudi Arabia was *not* made only because of their relative power in the Persian Gulf area; it was guided mainly by the perception that they were American "friends" and the major producers of oil. Hence, the twin-pillar policy contained the elements of both the older containment policy and the newer policy of the Guam Doctrine. For this reason, Iran and Saudi Arabia were regarded as American, and Iraq as Soviet, "surrogates" during the period between the 1968 announcement of British withdrawal from the Persian Gulf and the outbreak of the Arab-Israeli War of 1973.

Have the October War, the Arab oil embargo, the explosion of oil prices, and subsequent developments changed the American conception of the Middle East states? This question is of paramount importance, because it is widely believed that these revolutionary events changed the balance of power in favor of the Arab Middle East countries and OPEC. John G. Stoessinger goes so far as to claim that these events wrought a significant change in Kissinger's attitude toward all small states: "Kissinger's attention had been focused on the world's major power wielders."

The pawns on the global chessboard seemed quite expendable to him, until suddenly and without warning some of them decided to improve their lowly status. The Arab oil embargo and the demands for a "new international economic order" that swept through the Third World like a hurricane, convinced Kissinger that he finally would have to pay attention to the smaller nations of Africa, Latin America, and Asia.[122]

---

[122] John G. Stoessinger, *Henry Kissinger: The Anguish of Power* (New York: W. W. Norton, 1976), pp. 217, 220.

In light of my analysis, however, no overnight change in Kissinger's conception of the status of small states in international politics did in fact occur. Not only did he himself threaten military intervention in the Middle East oilfields (despite the rhetoric of "cooperation"), try to line up the consumer nations against the producers (despite the rhetoric of "interdependence"), and use American peacemaking efforts to lift the oil embargo (despite protestations to the contrary), but his advisers, such as Thomas O. Enders and William Simon, for example, went out of their way to denounce the OAPEC and OPEC nations, and Daniel P. Moynihan, at the UN, unfurled the ideological banner of "liberty" in opposition to the whole, allegedly socialist third world. Nor did some leading American scholars change their view of the international system and the place of small states in it, as evidenced, for example, by Robert Tucker's strong advocacy of U.S. military intervention in the Persian Gulf oilfields.

In the absence of any significant change in the traditional American conception of Middle East states even after the October War, the Ford Administration continued—despite mounting criticism—to react to fast-moving events, while invoking a hodge-podge of old and new concepts derived from the Truman Doctrine, the Guam Doctrine and detente to justify its policies in the Middle East. The ensuing dilemmas facing U.S. policymakers have not been resolved by the change of administration. The Carter Administration, like its predecessor, faces such problems as maintaining a "special relationship" with both Saudi Arabia and Israel at the same time; supporting Iran as an "ally" and criticizing it simultaneously over the price of oil; and reconciling arms sales to Saudi Arabia and Iran primarily for insuring security in the Persian Gulf, despite the clear probability of Saudi arms transfers to the Arab "confrontation" states in the event of a new Arab-Israeli war, and of Iranian military aid to Pakistan in a new Indo-Pakistani war. All these and related problems—such as the quantity and the level of sophistication of U.S. arms sales to regional states, the nonproliferation of nuclear weapons in the area, and the limitation of American and Soviet naval deployment in the Indian Ocean—will probably be more manageable if the mixture of older and newer conceptions of U.S. policy in the Middle East is transformed boldly into a new conception of *regional order by regional states*.

The formulation of such a new conception is made possible and desirable now, more than ever before, by two sets of new and important realities. First, *the Middle East states have emerged as important actors on the international economic and political scene, especially in South Asia and Africa.* Their emerging concern with the security of the Red Sea and the Horn of Africa is a recent example. Second, *the Middle East states have demonstrated beyond doubt that they are capable of containing the extension of Soviet power in the region directly, as in Egypt, and indirectly, as in the case of Oman where the*

Iranian intervention has helped to forestall the Dhofari radical movement. The former has enhanced the prospects of U.S. peacemaking efforts in the Arab-Israeli conflict, and the latter has strengthened the security of the Persian Gulf. In the meantime, U.S. commercial, economic and cultural ties with most states of the Middle East have improved at an unprecedented rate; the United States has been accepted as the most desirable intermediary power in the Arab-Israeli conflict; American personnel have become involved in the implementation of the Sinai accord; and the United States has been assisting in the social, economic and military development of regional states.

These new realities provide the Carter Administration with unprecedented opportunities for recognizing the Middle East states as the legitimate potential builders of their own future regional order. Neither the cold war conception of John Foster Dulles nor the great-power conception of Henry Kissinger allowed for such recognition. Given the realities of the rigid bipolar system of the time, the Dulles conception of the Middle East allowed for U.S. cooperation and alliance with only those regional states that were prepared to accept American clientization, for whatever reasons. The so-called nonaligned states of the region were beyond the pale of American patrimony. Kissinger's great-power conception of the international system left its mark even on the Guam Doctrine, to the extent that the doctrine called for the devolution of American responsibilities to only those regional states "friendly" to the United States. The doctrine, however, significantly called for American avoidance of the "impulses" of the Cold War era in light of the new realities of an emerging complex and fluid multipolar international system. Nevertheless, the devolution of responsibilities to the Persian Gulf states applied only to Iran and Saudi Arabia, and they are perceived today as American "surrogates." In a very real sense, the American "clients" of the Dulles era are now regarded as American "surrogates."

The new and bold American conception of the Middle East that this study calls for, however, will entail "declientization" of the "friendly" states and genuine acceptance of all major Middle East countries as partners of the United States in the construction of a stable regional order. The American partnership with Middle East states will be determined by their capabilities to contribute to this end rather than by their "special relationship" with the United States. This new conception will open up unprecedented opportunities for developing American relations with not only our old "friends," for example, Saudi Arabia, Iran and Israel, but also the newer ones such as Syria, and even Iraq before long. The importance of improved American-Syrian relations to regional order has already been demonstrated in the constructive role Syria has played in containing the adverse effects that the Lebanese civil war might have spilled over onto the rest of the region. In this way Syria has certainly assisted the American search for peace in the Middle East.

Achievement of the overriding goal of constructing order throughout the Middle East will serve to protect and promote American interests. It will also benefit the Middle East states. The survival and independence of the territorial state is the most fundamental (twin) goal of all Middle East countries. Yet the very shape of the region's state system itself remains largely unsettled. The reason for this is not the Arab-Israeli conflict, because that conflict itself is, in the last analysis, a reflection of the broader problem of the revolutionary conditions of the Middle East state system. That system was artificially carved out, largely by the requirements of European diplomacy in the wake of the disintegration of the Ottoman Empire at the end of World War I. It was never fully accepted before or after the attainment of independence by the new territorial states. It is plagued today not only by the Arab and Palestinian nonrecognition of the state of Israel and the Israeli occupation of Arab lands, but also by the ancient tension between the transnational vision of a united "Arab Nation" and the quest for the survival of the independent and separate territorial states.

So far American policy in the area has tended more to aggravate than alleviate the revolutionary conditions of the Middle East state system, because it has been preoccupied with the containment of Soviet power and influence. But a Middle East-oriented conception of American policy, as proposed in this study, will focus attention on this basic problem of regional order-building as an end in itself. Whether ultimately that order will be maintained through such mechanisms as a simple (two-state) or multiple balance of power, or a collective security system involving all Middle East states, or a combination of these, the important point is that such a conception of U.S. policy will entail more rather than less American partnership with the regional states in the foreseeable future. The United States is the most acceptable external power to mediate between the Arab states and Israel, and to assist in the construction of a regional order in the entire Middle East, with or without the cooperation of other great powers.

Just as this construction will assist in achieving a legitimate and stable external order among the Middle East states, it will have the potential of aiding the establishment of a stable and just order within Middle East societies. We can help in attaining the latter objective if we adopt what I call the "empirical empathic" approach to the study of Middle East foreign policy and society. Neither the great-power approach nor the so-called liberal-democratic ideology can provide a realistic understanding of the Middle East environment for American policymakers. For different reasons both approaches tend to look upon Middle East society excessively from the outside. One fails to perceive the realities of the

Middle East situation mainly because of preoccupation with the interests, objectives and courses of action of the great powers in the area, and the other equally fails to do so largely because the authoritarian nature of Middle East societies is found to be unpalatable to its ideology. Yet, as we have seen, the leaders of the area are preoccupied with internal control *not* so much as a matter of deliberate choice in favor of authoritarian control, but as a reflection of the revolutionary and unsettled conditions of their underdeveloped societies. The problem of war and peace in the Middle East also is inseparable from the internal volatility of Middle East societies as well as the revolutionary conditions of the Middle East state system.

Construction of a comprehensive regional order will go far to aid the creation of a more stable and just internal order, since the primary focus of concern will shift from the great powers to the regional powers, thus improving the chances for viewing these societies in their own terms. If so, this will foster the realization that external peace and domestic order must go hand in hand. Whether it is the civil war in Lebanon; or the political and economic upheaval in Egypt; or the rampant inflation and strikes, the scandals of the Labor Party, and the chronic gap between European and Oriental Jews in Israel; or the repeated terrorism and assassinations in Iran—the overriding fact of domestic life in all Middle East societies is the need for nonviolent political, social and economic change. The monopoly of economic and political power by minorities, whether the Maronite Christians in Lebanon, the Alawi Muslims in Syria, or the Farsi-speaking elite in Iran, will probably mean more rather than less authoritarian control in the foreseeable future.

The United States can neither control nor reverse these salient features of Middle East societies, but it can extend to them full partnership in their search for control over their own destiny. This is compatible with our long-run interests. American aid should be offered to these societies in the future not merely as a matter of political incentive and inducement, as in the case of Egypt for the conclusion of the Sinai agreement in 1975, but as a boost to the long-term goals of basic social and economic development. The availability of unprecedented capital resources in the oil-producing nations and the preference of these states for American technology have created unsurpassed opportunities for U.S. partnership with the Middle East states.

The search for a Middle East peace will probably prove illusory in the long run if it is pursued in the narrow context of trying to settle "essential issues," as proposed by the Carter Administration. That search could be made more meaningful if it becomes part of a comprehensive search for the construction of a more stable and just order in the entire Middle East.